MILLIONAIRE KIDS

Inspiring Stories of Young Entrepreneurs Who Became Rich Before Graduating High School

Emily Lin

ISBN: Paperback — 978-1-95-388456-5

Table of Contents

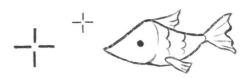

⇒—Introduction —➤

How do they do it? How do seemingly normal children and teenagers take simple ideas and turn them into million-dollar businesses? Is the secret to their success something innate or can it be learned and replicated by others? It's time to find out!

In this book, we'll take a look at the life-stories of children and teenagers, across the globe, who all saw opportunities in front of them and were brave enough to seize them. We'll also examine the pathway each young entrepreneur's life followed, discovering what gave them their ability to succeed despite their young age.

Each of the young people in this book showed true entrepreneurial spirit. However, they didn't all become wealthy by selling the same product or by using the same business plan. Therefore, this book will divide our young entrepreneurs' stories into five categories, which broadly cover the different paths that each of them took to become a millionaire. These categories are innovators, apps/websites, sales/marketing, food, and entertainment. These categories will not only add some structure to the book but will also allow you, the reader, to distinguish and compare the success of each young entrepreneur more thoughtfully.

Before we start looking at these young entrepreneurs' stories, I think it is important to restate that these children and teenagers are ordinary, everyday people. They are not the children of royalty or of billionaires, and they didn't have trust funds to fall back on or to use for funding their business. It *IS* true that not all of them came from impoverished backgrounds, and some of them had some help or support from their parents. However, none of them were helped to the point where it takes away their title of self-made millionaires.

Also by Inspired Publishing

- Amazing Stories for Special Girls: A Collection of Inspiring Lessons about Kindness, Confidence, and Teamwork

- Amazing Stories for Exceptional Boys: Inspiring Tales of Bravery, Friendship, and Self-Belief

- Interesting Stories for Curious Kids: An Amazing Collection of Unbelievable, Funny, and True Stories from Around the World!

- What Does That Mean?: Better Understand Idioms, Phrases, and Sayings | And Discover the Fascinating History Behind Their Origins

- Accidental Inventions That Changed Our World: 50 True Stories of Mistakes That Actually Worked and Their Origins

Get the Audiobook for Free!

If you enjoy listening to books while you're on the go, I have exciting news for you! You can download the audiobook version of "Millionaire Kids" absolutely free! Yes, completely free, simply by signing up for a 30-day trial on Audible at zero cost.

To begin, simply scan the QR code below.

Scan or visit -
www.booksbycooper.com/audible

Want Our Next Book For Free?

Simply enter your details on our sign-up page, and our next fun-filled book for kids will be yours to enjoy. It's easy, quick, and completely free. Don't miss out on this opportunity to add an exciting new book to your child's collection.

To begin, simply scan the QR code below.

Scan or visit - www.booksbycooper.com/next

SCAN ME

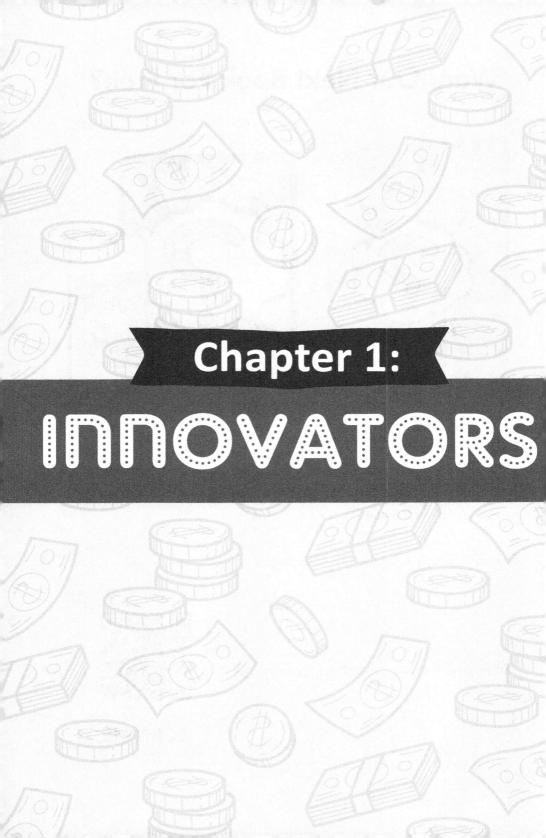

Chapter 1:
INNOVATORS

Kiowa Kavovit

Kiowa Kavovit made a massive splash in the world of business when she became the youngest entrepreneur ever to take on the sharks of ABC's Shark Tank and win. The seven-year-old took on her formidable foes with grace and knowledge and came out on top. Kiowa's appearance on ABC's Shark Tank was spellbinding and she effortlessly reeled in the notoriously elusive investors.

What idea could Kiowa have pitched that allowed her to scratch up an investment from the feared business sharks? It was nothing more than an ingenious take on the simple adhesive bandage.

At the age of four, Kiowa told her dad she didn't like the adhesive bandages that her parents and teacher used to fix those little boo-boos that all kids get. Kavovit wanted something that was prettier and easier to apply and – honestly – just more fun. From this conversation, Kiowa and her dad came up with the idea of a translucent liquid compound that Kiowa proudly named Boo Boo Goo. Boo Boo Goo can be painted or rolled onto any little boo-boo and will not come, off until it is peeled off. Best of all, the seven-year-old's innovation does not only come in dull flesh tones. It comes in a full range of colors, including fabulous pink, which we must all admit is far better than the adhesive bandages we have grown up with. And it's a lot prettier!

The sharks did point out that Boo Boo Goo is not the first roll-on adhesive plaster on the medical market. However, this didn't put them off, as they understood that Kiowa and her Boo Boo Goo were special. This was because Kiowa had access to an untouched and profitable market-base. As a seven-year-old, Kiowa had something no adult had, she was able to understand best what would attract others within her age group. She also understood that when seven-year-olds want something, they will most likely get it in the end, especially if it's functional.

Kiowa is lucky – as a young entrepreneur – to have Andrew Michael Kavovit as her dad. Like his daughter,

Andrew Kavovit is also an entrepreneur. He used his experience in the world of business and entrepreneurship to support his daughter after she entered Shark Tank. However, the seven-year-old only needed minimal help and guidance from her dad. She used her brilliant idea, her understanding of her target market, and her charm to secure a million-dollar investment from shark, Kevin O'Leary. His investment in Kiowa Kavovit's Boo Boo Goo got him a 25% share of the up-and-coming company (Cava, 2014).

And like any self-respecting entrepreneur, Kiowa is not finished. She has confirmed that Boo Boo Goo is only the first of the many innovative ideas she has in a mind full of new and improved products. She also has insight into which target market to pitch them. It is clear we have not heard the last of Kiowa, and many within the business world are excited to see what this pint-sized entrepreneur – who already has a million-dollar investment to her name – will come up with next.

Madison Robinson

Like a lot of children her age, Madison Robinson liked to draw. She also had a budding interest in fashion. In 2006, she found herself taking her flip flop and tracing it; and then she filled the drawing with an ocean-full of different sea creatures. Once she'd finished her fun drawing, she wanted to show off her creativity to her parents, like any other eight-year-old. She took her picture to her dad, and made a joke that she had created fish flops. Madison's pun was meant as nothing more than a silly little play on words, but it caught her dad's interest. So much so that he purchased the domain name FishFlop. com in case Madison ever decided to make something out of her fishy pun.

From the outside looking in, it seemed that Madison's fishy joke would come to nothing. To those around her she seemed to be a normal kid – maybe even a little nerdy . She certainly didn't come across as someone with a million-dollar plan brewing in her back pocket. However, as Madison grew up, so did her love for fashion and her entrepreneurial vision. She worked with her dad to get some of her FishFlops transformed, from crayons and paper, into actual wearable flip-flops.

The outside world's first view of Madison's entrepreneurial talent occurred when Madison took some real-life FishFlops to a local trade show, when she was just 12 years old. Madison already knew that, if she wanted her FishFlops idea to become more than just a pocket money endeavor, she needed to break into the mainstream clothing industry. To do this, the 12-year-old bravely wrote a letter to a buyer at Nordstrom, in July of 2012. this led to sixty-four of Nordstrom's stores agreeing to sell Madison's FishFlops.

Madison continued to show her expertise as an entrepreneur, making sure that her achievements were well-publicized, as well as making sure that everyone her age knew about them. Her media-savvy plan resulted in an avalanche of emails from other retail outlets that wanted to stock Madison's fish-foot friends, including Macy's.

When Madison was 16, her success as a businesswoman was rewarded, after she won the 2014 Principles of Business, Marketing, and Finance Award. Madison continues to work on new and fun ways to expand her business and ensures to ensure that the products she sells remain relevant and interesting to her target market. She continues to use the media, especially social media, to promote her company's products, which now include t-shirts, hats, and phone-covers.

Emily Matson and Julianne Goldmark

Similar to many girls in the early 2000s, best friends, Emily Matson and Julianne Goldmark, were obsessed with the television program, Gossip Girl, and the trendy fashions that it showcased. Who wouldn't want to look like Blair Waldorf?

What's more, the friends attended a school that required them to wear a boring school uniform, which meant that when they got to wear casual clothes, they wanted to make sure they expressed themselves as much as they could while still following the latest trends. This combination of an obsession with the fashion of Gossip Girl and a need for a personalized creative outlet inspired them to create some simple hair accessories, which would make them millionaires before they even graduated high school.

At fourteen, the two friends were out looking for fabric that they could use to create Gossip Girl-inspired headwear, but which would not damage their hair or create kinks in it. The friends settled on breathable satin. They were soon the envy of many other girls in their school. The friends realized they had opportunity before them, an so they got together each weekend to create and sew different styles of the headwear that they could sell to other friends and classmates.

Emily and Julianne understood that one of the most effective ways to establish a business is to have a good brand-identity. The friends used their friendship as the cornerstone of their business and decided to combine shortened versions of their names to create the name of their business; they called it Emi-Jay.

The two friends continued to make their hair accessories on the weekend and to sell them, making themselves a little pocket money to spend. Then, one day, it all changed, after Jennifer Aniston was spotted on the red carpet wearing one of the girls' creations. Emily's mom had given hair stylist,

Chris MacMillian, one of her daughter's creations on a whim. As luck would have it, Chris MacMillian loved the accessory, and Emi-Jay was just what was needed to finish off his look for Jennifer Aniston's red carpet appearance.

Thanks to Jennifer Aniston's patronage, the girls' headwear accessories became a must-have item for fourteen-year-old girls and indeed for anyone who wanted to be someone. Retail outlets across the United States began competing to sell the girls' products in their stores, with the girls' accessories eventually being available to purchase in over 3,000 stores across the US.

The young entrepreneurs understood that their success was closely linked to their insight to brand themselves well and their connection to Jennifer Aniston's red-carpet appearance. They took these two realizations and ran with them, ensuring they used any media exposure to attract interest in their products. The friends partnered with celebrities, such as Gigi Hadid and Kim Kardashian, to promote their products and set up partnerships with social media influencers to broaden their target base.

As the years went on and the two friends grew up, so did their company. Today, they continue to ensure that the products they sell keep up with relevant fashion trends. Emily and Julianne still like to draw on popular TV shows for inspiration, just as they did when it all started.

Brennan Agranoff

I n 2013, Brennan Agranoff was just 13 years old. However, despite his young age, Brennan succeeded in spotting a need for customized sports clothing amongst his friends. It was a gap in the market for which no one seemed able to provide a solution. Brennan quickly decided that he might also be the right person to find a solution to this need. He did this by founding HoopSwagg, a company that created personalized sports clothes.

Brennan was able to take on the challenge of HoopSwagg's creation, thanks to his supportive parents, who, gave him guidance, but – ultimately – allowed him to make his own decisions, even those they thought were risky. Brennan's parents wanted him to learn how best to be an adult, but they didn't want to shelter him. They saw that the most effective way for him to develop was by learning through his own mistakes. In other words, making decisions and learning from the outcome, whether it was good or bad.

Brennan's company grew steadily. By the time he was 17, he was the CEO of a company that had made him a millionaire. Brennan believes that to be a good entrepreneur, you need to be connected to the product or service you are selling to your target market. If you want your business to be successful, you must have a vested interest that is more than just the money you get out of it; you honestly need to care about what you're doing.

Brennan attributes much of his entrepreneurial success to the social interactions he has in his day-to-day life. These interactions not only allow him to talk about and promote his products, but it also means that he is continually connecting with people who inspire him to have new ideas and to develop new ways of marketing products. This business approach has gained Brennan a vast amount of respect within his local community. Those around him see that even though his company is a global entity, he is still a local Portland boy who is very respectful and always looking to help his community by fundraising for the charities within it.

Brennan could have stopped working with HoopSwagg in 2017, after already accomplishing a level of financial success that few others have obtained. That was also this year that he was named Baylor University's Teen Entrepreneur of the Year. However, Brennan was not done as an entrepreneur Brennan and, in 2018, he created the brand PetParty. Like its older sibling, HoopSwagg, PetParty is all clothing and product customization. Unlike HoopSwagg, PetParty is not only for humans. The company allows people to personalize different products for both themselves and their pets. It allows people to personalize various products with images of their oh-so-cute pets. So, although he was already a millionaire well before the age of 18, PetParty added to Brennan's business portfolio, bringing in $2.4 million in sales (Content Hacker™, 2022).

Brennan's success story has been the focus of many news articles in well-established business magazines, such as *Forbes* and *Entrepreneur*. They are all fascinated by Brennan and his dive-into-the-deep-end, no-holding-back approach to business and life. As an entrepreneur, Brennan is not afraid to take a chance. He understands that most people are never successful in business because they are too scared to try something new. People need to see that a business venture may look like a gamble, but it only looks that way because it requires you to try something different.

Moziah Bridges

Growing up, Moziah Bridges wanted to be styling. For most young kids, that would mean having the latest sneakers and the coolest hoodie, but not for Moziah. All he wanted was a well-tailored suit jacket and a classy bow tie. Moziah attributed his desire for elegant clothing to his dad, who always wore suits even if he was chilling at home. The biggest issue facing Moziah in his pursuit of the fancier things in life was cost. His mom had no problem with her nine-year-old wanting to dress on the smarter side of smart-casual, but she was not willing to fork out the expense needed for the clothing items he required, especially not for bow ties.

Enter Moziah's grandmother, who just so happened to have worked her entire life as a seamstress. That allowed Moziah to do something not many nine-year-old boys would do; instead of just asking his grandmother to make some bow ties for him, Moziah asked her to teach him how to sew them. He then combined his newly developed sewing skills with some online research. Moziah looked to see if anyone was selling high-quality yet affordable bow ties and soon discovered that no one was. It seemed he could be just the boy to fill the gap in this niche market.

Like many entrepreneurs, Moziah started selling his homemade products on Etsy, under the branding Mo's Bows. Whenever a bow tie was ordered from the company, it came with the personal assurance that either Moziah or his mom had made it. This assurance continues to this day; Moziah understands that it is this homemade and personal touch that adds to the appeal of Mo's Bows.

In 2015, and at the age of eleven years old, Moziah realized that if he wanted to grow his business, he would need the backing and investment of more established business people. So, along with his mom, Moziah entered ABC's Shark Tank to pitch his already established business to the formidable sharks.

Moziah walked into the dreaded Shark Tank asking for an investment of $50,000 for a 20% stake in Mo's Bows. That is what he walked away with after gaining the support of Daymond John (Shark Tank, 2014). The young entrepreneur enthralled Daymond; he could see that Moziah truly cared about the business he had founded and was willing to step up and work hard to make his company grow. However, Daymond did something far more significant than simply investing in Moziah's company; he took Moziah under his wing and began to mentor the young entrepreneur. Daymond shared his years of business savvy with the young man, and helped him discover opportunities to promote his business that Moziah would not have been able to find on his own. The same year as Moziah appeared on Shark Tank, he also served as a fashion correspondent for the NBA draft and appeared in Time Magazine's list of The 30 Most Influential Teens. Moziah continued to have a fantastic year, in 2015, when he attended the inaugural White House Demo Day. He was able to give the then-president, Barack Obama, some fashion help at the event, by presenting him with a specially made Obama Blue bowtie. In 2017, the NBA cemented their partnership with Moziah, by making his custom-made neckwear an essential item of all 30 NBA teams.

Even though his business was a success, Moziah continued to go to school, working hard to graduate well and to ensure that he continued to lay a good foundation for his future in the business world. Moziah's determination to dress well and help others do the same paid off, and he was a well-established millionaire before he graduated high school.

Abbey Fleck

People all over the world would probably agree that bacon is one of the most delicious foods in the world. This delicious treat can be cooked in many ways, but there is one method that trumps them all; crispy. However, bacon needs to be cooked just right to get the correct level of crispy goodness, and preferably with a minimal amount of effort. This thought was what spurred Abbey Fleck into action – as well as an offhand comment from her dad, about how he loved extra crispy bacon but hated of all the unhealthy fat that came with it. Abbey shut herself away to devise an innovative way to get crispy bacon while letting all the unwanted fat drip off and without having to use paper towels to soak it up.

What is so extraordinary is that when Abbey decided to solve her dad's problem, she was only eight years old. She worked hard to find a microwave-safe, inexpensive dish that could be made to get bacon as crispy as possible while getting rid of all of the unhealthy fat. After a relatively short time, Abbey came back to her dad with the Makin' Bacon® dish, a simple, square, inch-deep container made from microwave plastic with three T-shaped holders in the center. Abbey had seemingly thought of everything when she designed her new bacon cooker. She made sure that it was user-friendly and easy to store, and ensured that her Makin' Bacon® dish was inexpensive, at a mere $7.

Abbey knew that if she wanted her efforts to pay off, she would need to make sure that as many crispy-bacon lovers as possible found out about her new fantastic Makin' Bacon® dish. She did this, in 1994, with the help of her dad, who went along with her to meet the executives at Armour bacon. Abbey and her dad negotiated a which launched a promotional campaign that pushed their bacon and Abbey's new Makin' Bacon®. Armour and Abbey's promotional campaign saw the young entrepreneur appear on many TV programs, including The Oprah Winfrey Show and Late Night with David Letterman. The media storm created by Armour's promotional campaign and the quality of Abbey's product meant that sales of the Makin' Bacon® soared.

Thanks to Abbey's ability to see a need and to find a way to fill it, she made herself a millionaire well before the age of 18. What is more, her success was not short-lived, as the Makin' Bacon® is still available for purchase on Amazon.com and in Walmart stores.

Noa Mintz

Most of us have heard of The Babysitters Club, the children's books, and now there is a Netflix series about a group of young girls who start a babysitting business together. Little did we all know that Noa Mintz is the real-life version of those stories. Like the characters in the stories, Noa also had a strong entrepreneurial streak, and she was always talking to her mom about how she needed to be more money-savvy, or how she could make more money if she worked for herself.

Growing up, Noa's friend's little sisters all wanted to have Noa babysit them; Noa was just so much fun. She always came up with the most exciting activities and even knew how to make a rainy day inside fun. The native New Yorker, who lived in upper Manhattan, also knew all the most incredible places in the city that were kid-friendly. When Noa was only 12, she decided to combine all of the advice she had given her mom with her talent for making little kids happy, and to use her school holiday to come up with a business plan.

The business plan Noa created was about looking for nannies who shared the qualities she had. They had to be fun and caring, and they needed to be able to keep kids entertained and happy. They also had to provide kids with structure and help them grow and learn. They needed to work alongside the parents to make sure that the kids they were looking after got all they needed to succeed. It was a tall order, but Noa felt that it would be possible. When she was happy with her business plan, she presented it to her dad, who works in private equity. He was thoroughly impressed by his daughter's idea and the plan she had put together. He agreed to help her out where he could, and to give her guidance when she asked for it. Nora named her new business Nannies by Noa.

The first nannies that Noa brought on to work for her business were older sisters of friends or people from the gym she went to with her mom. Noa and the nannies she hired impressed the clients they had, and word-of-mouth meant that Noa's little business became increasingly popular and not so little anymore. By 2015, Nora had a network of 25 full-time nannies and 50 babysitters, who worked with around 190 different families. The company made money by taking a small percentage of the money earned by each nanny and babysitter and the system worked well for all of the parties involved. The nannies and babysitters had a stable client base and were ensured regular work, the families knew they could trust the people looking after their kids, and Noa made money doing something that brought her joy.

As Noa moved further on in high school and the workload grew heavier, her business continued to grow as well and this required her to spend more time on it. Noa knew she had to take a step back, so that she could focus on school. To ensure that her business didn't suffer from her absence and that her hard work wasn't wasted, Noa promoted Allison Johnson, a trained social worker, to the role of CEO. Allison had started out as a nanny and she had already demonstrated her dedication and understanding of the business's vision, which impressed Nora and made her comfortable about giving Allison the position. Although Allison was now CEO, Noa kept up to speed with the business, checking in regularly with Allison to ensure that all was running smoothly.

Noa's hard work and vision paid off. She created an outstanding, thriving business that helped hundreds of families and allowed many, many kids to have fun-filled days and nights being looked after by people who cared deeply for them. Nora's entrepreneurial vision served her well, and she made herself a millionaire before graduating high school.

Gabrielle Jordan

Gabrielle Jordan's foray into the entrepreneurial world began when she was only nine years old. She had started watching YouTube tutorials and crafting jewelry two years prior to that and then turned her hobby into a full-fledged business. In 2009, she founded Jewelz of

Jordan in Maryland, a fashion jewelry outlet that initially focused on mother-daughter matching sets. Friends and family members were the first customers of the store until Gabrielle started vending at seminars and workshops. She launched the online store in 2011. Today at twenty years of age, Gabrielle is a Computer-Aided Designing and Management (CAD/CAM) certified jewelry designer and alumnus of the well-known Gemological Institute of America (GIA), London. Jewelz of Jordan has currently attained the status of a luxury brand. Her clientele includes Columbia University, Syracuse University, Google, United Way, the United States Embassy Nassau–The Bahamas, and the Congressional Black Caucus. You'd ask, "What more could a girl ask for?" A lot more, as it turns out!

Even before she entered her teens, Gabrielle became a motivational speaker for Girl Scouts and other youth entrepreneurship events. She realized how many other girls, though endowed with talents like her, were unaware of the opportunities to carve a successful career path. Out of her experiences in business and her desire to motivate people of her age, was born the bestseller *The Making of a Young Entrepreneur: A Kids Guide to Developing the Mind-Set for Success*—2011. This book has sold over 10,000 copies worldwide as of today and was No. 1 on Amazon. Subsequently, she has been a speaker on platforms such as TEDx and Inbound.

Since 2011, almost every year in Gabrielle's life calendar has been punctuated by one or more of her achievements. She was awarded the 2011 Rising Star Young Entrepreneur of the Year by the Entrepreneur and Professional Network

(EPNET). In the same year, she was also declared *One of the Most Influential Community Leaders* by Sharpermind Consultants and by Mayor Stephanie Rawling-Blake of the city of Baltimore. She was the first recipient of the annual EPNET Young Entrepreneur Scholarship Award. 2012 saw her receive the Greater Prince George's Business Roundtable Outstanding CEO Award. In 2013, she was a Black Enterprise Teenpreneur finalist. In 2014 she was the recipient of McDonald's 365Black Community Choice Award. 2015 was a turning point in her career as she was recognized as one of the INC. 5 Entrepreneurial Kids Who Basically Won the Internet, and she also won the Black Girls Rock M.A.D. Girl Award. Gabrielle was included among The Root Young Futurists of 2016. She was featured among *Teen Vogue*'s 21 Under 21, Magic Johnson's 32 Under 32, and Prince George's County Forty Under 40 lists in 2017. In 2018, she won the Millennial On The Rise Spectrum Circle Award (Jordan, 2019). She is breaking barriers even as we speak.

Being an entrepreneur and an author wasn't enough for Gabrielle. She founded the ExCEL Youth Mentoring Institute, which offers online mentoring programs for young people seeking to embrace leadership and entrepreneurial roles. Gabrielle herself being a product of various kinds of schooling—home, public, private, trading, and university—is a vociferous proponent of alternative forms of schooling. Her mentorship institute provides materials and resources for the youth who would like to educate themselves. She has engaged with thousands of young people, women, and children via her interviews, talks, as well as her institute.

If earlier she used to voice her opinions through radio talk shows, she is today a podcaster. Her *UV Effect* podcast draws on her personal experiences in researching her own past and helping to identify an individual's *Unique Value (UV)*, which would contribute to their innate sense of purpose. She has also been featured on several prestigious media platforms and shows, such as *The Harry Show*, TLC, and *The Huffington Post*.

Gabrielle Jordan does not intend to rest on her multiple laurels. She has been nothing less than a visionary in recognizing what the youth truly needs. Her creative talents and her unique gift of being able to articulate the thoughts and ideals of leadership skills make her an outstanding specimen among millennials. Her chutzpah and gusto are what has granted her the proverbial Midas touch, so to speak—the ability to turn whatever she touches into gold.

Chapter 2:

APPS/ WEBSITES

Robert Nay

December 22 2010, marked the day that Robert Nay's life changed forever. It was on that day that the number one iPhone game app, Bubble Ball, was released.

In 2010, Robert Nay was in grade eight and, while his friends were goofing off and playing PlayStation, watching TV, or shooting hoops, Robert was painstakingly working out how to create a game app for the Apple iStore; a game he hoped that millions of iPhone users would download and play.

What is truly remarkable is that when Robert developed Bubble Ball, he had no formal training in computer programming. Roberts's computer abilities were completely self-taught. He first stepped into the world of programming in grade three, when he created a simple website for himself. Then, in middle school, Robert began to teach himself how to code using a Corona program. He found that he was proficient enough to create a few simple games that could be played on iPod Touches. Robert would later use Corona as the platform upon which he created Bubble Ball.

To an outsider, Robert might have looked like a natural at coding and they might think that he had taken to it like a fish to water; however, this was not the case. He has said that he struggled to grasp the concept of coding. He believes his success in it is due only to his determination not to give up and to keep trying to understand what he did wrong each time he failed.

When Robert released his game to the iPhone app store, it became an overnight success. The game was intensely addictive, and lured players in with its multi-levels. Those who played it were fooled at first, because it seemed to be a relatively straightforward and easily mastered game. However, as the player progressed into the levels, they were met with more and more challenging objectives, which seemingly asked the player to bend the laws of physics to reach the finish line. Bubble Ball was so popular when it was released that it soon became the number one downloaded game – an astonishing six million times – surpassing even Angry Birds. Its popularity was primarily attributed to Roberts's smart marketing choice; he made his game free of charge, meaning it was more accessible than most iPhone games at that time. The millions of downloads meant that fourteen-year-old Robert made himself $2 million within the first two weeks of Bubble Ball's being available on the app store, (Bruce, 2015). Robert did not earn this money from those who downloaded his game, but rather from the advertising space within the game's set-up.

Robert used his entrepreneurial abilities to create an income for himself without deterring customers with a hefty price tag. He continues to work in the programming and coding industry and has developed and helped to create many other games in the past few years. He also went on to obtain some formal training in programming, by studying computer science at Brigham Young University.

Jack Bloomfield

It would seem that Jack Bloomfield was born an entrepreneur; he always seemed to have some new business venture in his pocket. He started by selling sweets to his friends or mowing the lawns of people in his neighborhood. He used the money he made from those enterprises to help fund his adventure into the world of programming and coding. His money was well spent, as he created his first app at only 12 years old. Jack's app earned him a respectable amount of money, but he had not yet made his first million.

When Jack turned 15, he began to take an interest in e-commerce, thanks to some financial YouTube videos he had been watching. He saw a need for online stores that sold gimmicky niche products. Jack used his own entrepreneurial ideas, and those he had learned from fellow entrepreneurs within the digital realm, to develop the five websites he had created into a fully established company. This brought in enough profit to make Jack a multi-millionaire before the end of his high school career.

At the same time, the media has played a definitive role in promoting Jack and his entrepreneurial success. He has been featured in countless magazines and has appeared on various TV shows. However, he is very adept at keeping the ideas and plans that made him an e-commerce master close to his chest.

At 18, Jack turned his skillset toward the world of computers and e-commerce, to help tackle the issue of online fraud, which costs the United States around $29 billion a year (Leonhardt, 2021). Jack created a system, known as Disputify, that scans online money transactions. It detects fraudulent transactions in real-time and gives online shoppers and sellers greater peace of mind. It's feeling of assurance is well founded, as Disputify has already prevented over $10 million worth of fraudulent transactions (Bloomfield, 2019).

Jack's success in the business world brought him membership of the Australian Institute of Company

Directors and, to-date, he is their youngest member. Jack also understands that not all of those in his neighborhood, city, and country have had the opportunities he has had. This has led to his donating a large amount of both his time and wealth to supporting the growth of real-world skills' education within the school system. Jack has also created a program in which budding entrepreneurs can enroll. The program doesn't tell students all of Jacks' secrets to success, but they will be taught how to think outside of the box, to come up with their own path to business success.

Adam Hildreth

Adam Hildreth was born in 1985, in Leeds, and entered his teens in the 1990s. As a teenager in the 1990s, Adam spent a lot of time on the internet. Unfortunately, in these early stages of internet popularity, there were very few websites where teenagers could have coherent social interactions. Seeing this need, Adam decided not to wait for someone else to fill it; rather, he would try to fill it himself.

At 14, Adam worked on the concept of a social website with some of his friends. They pooled their ideas, making sure that the website had enough different features so that any teen who went on it would find something they enjoyed. Adam and his group named the site Dubit. Adam left school at 16, to work full-time on the project. Looking back, many people hailed the creation of this site as one of the first true social media platforms.

The website quickly became one of the most popular sites in the United Kingdom. It was so popular, in fact, that in the year of its launch, Adam and his friends entered the Guinness Book of World Records, as the youngest directors of a company in the United Kingdom. Their website soon made the boys multi-millionaires. Their friends continued working on it, adapting it to fit the changing target market, and bringing in digital gaming when it became popular and live games. The site also hosted mass live events for Metaverse, Roblox, Minecraft, and Core.

Adams' hard work and vision for both the present and future paid off. He showed what can be done when people fill the need they see in front of them. In 2014, the Sunday Times Rich list estimated Adam's wealth at £24 million, and given Adam's career trajectory, it was predicted that he would be worth £40 million by 2020.

Ashley Qualls

Ashley Qualls was just an ordinary teenage girl. In fact, some might even have said that she started life off on the wrong foot; having been raised by a single parent who often struggled to provide for the family. Those misfortunes didn't stop Ashley from seeing an opportunity and having the courage to grasp it. She understood that life is not fair and that when you have the chance to make something out of what you have been given, you need to take it. Little did Ashley know, when she took the opportunity life gave her, that it would help her become one of the most successful young entrepreneurs in the world, as well as a millionaire, and all before leaving high school.

Ashley understood what it meant to struggle. She wanted to create a safe online platform for others like her to connect and hang out. She also wanted to give those, who like her were unsure of what the future held, inspiration. She wanted to show them that they could achieve great things despite their initial lack of skills or strategies. She wanted the platform to be a happy space, where people felt they could be open about their struggles and maybe even help each other as they all journeyed into the future together. However, if Ashley was to do this she needed a small investment, so her first investor was her mom, who lent her $8 so that she could purchase the domain name Whateverlife.com.

Before Ashley launched Whateverlife.com, she spent some time learning programming and web design to ensure that her website looked inviting. She created portfolios and graphics and, once she was happy with what she had made, Ashley opened up Whateverlife.com to the public, when she was 14 years old. The website found a strong audience of teenagers who, like Ashley, needed a safe space to hang out without the pressure of their daily lives.

Within a few months of the website's going live, Ashley had earned herself $70,000 and was able to pay her mom back the $8 she had lent her (ABCNews, 2007). Along with her wealth Ashley felt a newfound sense of confidence. She also saw that she could use what she had learned while creating her website. She began posting tutorials, showing her online friends and followers how they could create and develop different graphics and profiles, just as she had. Ashley attracted a great deal of interest in her tutorials, so she decided to modify Whateverlife.com to allow those with an account to upload the different projects they had created, thanks to her tutorials. This modification to the website helped grow the users' investment in the website, especially after Ashley added a feature that rewarded account holders for uploading with points, which could then be used to buy digital goods. These two modifications pushed the website's visits up to 300,000 a day. Growth like this meant that the website soon began to compete for daily views with other, bigger websites, such as cbsnews.com and oprah.com.

When Ashley was 16, her website was so popular that it drew the attention of Myspace co-founder, Brad Greenspan, who was blown away by Ashley's business sense and passion. Brad saw Ashley for what she was, a truly remarkable entrepreneur. However, despite Brad's admiration for the young entrepreneur, he realized that her website was a threat to his own. For that reason, he twice offered her a large amount of money in exchange for the rights to her website's domain name, but she refused. Many people could not understand why Ashely wouldn't sell her domain name to Brad and just take the money, which was well over $1,000,000.

Even without accepting the offer from the Myspace co-founder, Ashley was able to buy a house for herself and her family at the age of 16. By 2007, visits to Ashley's website had reached seven million, by the time she was 17, Ashley – the girl who thought she had no future – had become a completely self-made millionaire.

Ben Pasternak

At 16 years old, Australian-born Ben Pasternak accomplished what many adult entrepreneurs spend their entire lives working towards. Ben created an online company that gave its users the means to buy and sell their new or used products more effectively, and he called it Flogg Inc. He successfully pitched this business idea to Silicon Valley investors, and secured their support for his entrepreneurial plan. He then left his high school, his hometown, and even his country to move to New York. Ben was the living embodiment of what so many people chase and which always seems just out of reach; the "American Dream."

With the investment capital that he secured from his Silicon Valley instructors, and no more school homework to do, Ben was able to devote all of his time to his fledgling start-up, one that would soon make him the CEO of some of the biggest up-and-coming companies.

Although Flogg Inc. was Ben's most successful entrepreneurial venture, it was by no means his first. The teen was developing and creating game apps for Apple, when he was 14. While these games didn't bring him the financial success of his first start-up, they did lay the groundwork he needed for what was to come.

One of the apps Ben created grew quickly and spent time at the top of the Apple app store charts. This success put Ben's entrepreneurial abilities on the map. He was quickly accredited by companies, such as Google and Facebook. Apple also offered him a scholarship to attend their Worldwide Developers Conference. Unfortunately, even though Flogg Inc. helped Ben become an up-and-comer in the entrepreneurial world, its success was short-lived. After spending some time at the top of the download charts, it was then closed down due to a lack of profitability.

Even though Flogg Inc. had been taken down, Ben was not done by any means. He was in New York now, and running in the tech development circles he needed to be able to develop and find funding for his next app. This was Monkey, and it allowed teenagers from all over the world to video chat with people who shared the same interests as they had. Like Flogg Inc., Monkey became extremely popular in a short span of time. Ben used this popularity to secure a buyout from the social networking company Holla, who acquired the rights to the app for a large but undisclosed sum of money. Ben was 17 years old when he brokered this deal and sources close to him disclosed that he had definitely broken into the millionaire bracket with its sale.

With Monkey sold off, Ben moved on to his next venture, SIMULATE. What is different about SIMULATE is that it is not an app or a website. SIMULATE are vegetarian chicken nuggets and frankfurters. While this jump from app development to selling vegetarian products may seem nonsensical, it points us to the crux of Ben's entrepreneurial success, his ability to understand what is popular at the moment and what product – whether physical or online – has the largest target market.

Juliette Brindak

In 2005, when Juliette Brindak was just 16 years old, she launched her first website, called Miss O and Friends. She created the website from childhood drawings that she had done when she was ten years old. The drawings first came to life on a long road trip back home from a vacation that Juliette had taken with her family. She drew different pictures of a bunch of girls she called the "cool girls." Juliette's mom, who was a designer, was impressed by the drawings and helped Juliette turn them into different characters. They made one for Juliette and one for her little sister, Olivia. The characters returned when Olivia turned eight, and her mom had huge cardboard cutouts of the characters made, even adding some for the girls' friends. As Juliette grew older, she treasured those memories of the characters she and her mom had made and the carefree hours she, her sister, and their friends had spent playing with them.

These happy memories became even more important to hold on to, as Juliette grew older and began to interact on various social media sites. She soon found out that not everyone was kind when they were hiding behind a computer screen. Girls she had thought were friends were now acting in ways that hurt those around them. Social media was a place where you had to prove yourself worthy of friendship through your popularity rather than your personality and your kindness. Juliette had discovered online bullying, and she experienced firsthand how real and disheartening the issue could be. She also had to deal with the vast amount of long-lasting pain that could come with it.

With her childhood memories in mind, she decided to create a safe space, where she and her friends could hang out on online. She knew that if she was going to do this, she would need the help of a programming and coding specialist, whom she sourced and got to help her create what she needed. However, Juliette also began to learn how to code herself, so that she could be as involved as possible in the creation and running of her new safe online space. She freely admits that learning to code was not easy, and it took her hours of practice, but she is so thankful she took the time.

Juliette's website began to take shape, in partnership with outsourced programmers and her own creating and coding contributions. The website was a vibrant and fun space full of countless ways to interact and connect with friends. She also set it up so that those who tried to bully others would be warned and then removed if they chose not to learn from their mistakes or to change how they interacted with others.

The positive atmosphere of Miss O and Friends was captivating for teenage girls, and the site's popularity grew in leaps and bounds. Its attractiveness was so high that not only teenage girls were interested in it, but also large corporations and other social media sites. Procter and Gamble were one of those corporations, and they worked hard to strike a deal with Juliette, to allow then to invest in the website and to help to promote it; thus broadening its reach. At the same time as Procter and Gamble were considering investing in Juliette and her website, they evaluated it and valued it at $15 million (Business Insider, 2012).

John Magennis

John Magennis was born in 1981 in Boston, Massachusetts. He grew up with four older sisters and his parents. Like most teens in the 1990s, John spent much of his time on the internet. However, unlike other teenagers, John didn't just surf the internet; he helped to create it.

Today, if you want to create a website, you don't need to know anything about coding or programming. All you have to do is go to one of the many cookie-cutter websites that help you create a website from the many templates they offer. However, this was not the case in the 1990s and this is where John came in. He had learned how to work on computers at a young age, including learning about coding and programming. At 16, John decided to use his skills to help him earn a little pocket money. Both of his parents were business owners, which had a significant impact on John. It gave him a good understanding of what might be needed to start his own business. It also provided him with insight into how much work he would have to put into his business if he wanted it to be a success.

John posted an advert, offering his services to those who needed a website but who didn't know how to create one themselves. When he started out, he charged his client's $15 to make them a personalized website that was customized to their needs. He was still in school, and all of his creating-website work had to be done after school; so, he had to learn how to juggle schoolwork and his budding business. The websites John created for his clients were well-designed and user-friendly. John and his skills began to attract attention that impacted positively on his client base, which kept growing. Because of the high demand for his coding and programming abilities, John learned he could charge more for a customized website, sometimes as much as $30,000 (Weaver, 2015). Thanks to John's website creating skills, he became a self-made millionaire before he was 18.

Catherine Cook

I am sure we all understand the anxiety of being the new kid on the block. We know what it's like to show up at a party, a new school, or a camp and not have a friend to buddy up with. Catherine Cook found herself being flung into this same uncomfortable situation, after she moved to the town of Skillman, New Jersey with her family. Fourteen-year-old Catherine found herself in a new high school with no one but her brother to hang out with. They decided to look at the school's past yearbooks to see if they could learn anything about the teenagers they were going to school with, and to discover whether there were any connections between themselves and their school fellows that they could use to form friendships. They were disappointed, to say the least. The yearbooks had little to no relatable information in them about the school's students, and it looked as if Catherine and her brother had hit a dead end.

Or had they? Catherine began to think about how cool it would be if each student had the ability to fill out their section of the yearbook with all the information they wanted other people to know about them. This idea and Catherine's desire for new connections led to her coming up with a plan to create a website, called Myyearbook. com. It would be a space where high school students could connect, hang out and create their own personalized yearbooks.

Catherine did not write the code that created the website herself; she sourced an external developer to help her develop her dream site. She spent many hours talking with the developer to ensure that her site would be appealing to her target market and that it would be fun and easy to use. She promoted her website excitedly; for example, she created t-shirts advertising the website, in order to ensure that everyone in her town knew about Myyearbook.com and understood what it was all about. She also wanted to be certain they knew what they might gain by becoming a part of it. It worked, as 400 people joined the website in the first week of its being open.

Catherine received loads of positive feedback about the site, with one friend commenting on how it had become her new favorite way to procrastinate. Catherine continued to work hard to get her website's name and message out there, even reaching teens who didn't live in Skillman. This meant long hours of extra work for the teen; she had to learn quickly how to balance her school work and her business, which she admitted was not easy and she said that her school work often suffered because of her dedication to making Myyearbook.com a success.

The site's popularity grew as teens from all over joined up. Soon, large companies saw an opportunity to reach a younger demographic with targeted advertising campaigns. As an example, Paramount Films began to advertise on the site, spending up to $500,000 for space on Myyearbook.com. These adverts made Catherine well over a million dollars before she had even graduated high school.

Nick D'Aloisio

Nick D'Aloisio began coding and working in computer programming at the age of 12. He was fascinated by the world of smartphones and the possibilities contained within them. He started his programming journey with a basic iPhone development kit and never looked back.

As Nick grew older, it seemed evident that he would fall in love with the computer programming world as well. He had always loved breaking down, picking apart, and understanding large amounts of data, which was the mindset that perfectly fit the world of computers and software programming.

As Nick's understanding of how apps and software worked grew, he became more interested in the sentiment analysis of apps. Sentiment analysis (sometimes called opinion mining) is a technique that is used to determine whether data is positive, negative or neutral. Nick studied sentiment analysis on the sites he had created himself, as well as those others that were available on his iPhone. He did all he could to take in as much information as possible about the different coding languages used and sought out the best techniques to learn them. He used iTunes University as his main fountain of knowledge, but – unfortunately – sometimes even Apple failed to answer Nicks' questions. This often meant that Nick had to reach out to others for help, something that many people his age, or even older, struggle to do. However, Nick did not suffer from shyness, and he realized that if he didn't understand how something worked or why it worked a specific way, the best way to get an answer was to ask an expert, regardless of how famous they might be.

Nick continued to tinker away at programming and app building until, at 16, he struck an app gold mine after he created Summly. This ingenious app created summaries of the contents of web pages and search results, and put the content into simplified blocks of information that are easy to take in quickly. When it was first created, it was used to condense reviews, news, and reference pages. Nick was studying for school exams when the idea for the app came to him. He found that the information he was getting from his internet searches contained too much irrelevant information. He wanted a way of getting to the information he needed without wasting time by reading through all the 'other stuff'.

Summly was such a remarkable idea that the app, which achieved over 100,000 downloads when it first went live, attracted the attention of Hong Kong-based businessman and billionaire, Li Ka-Shing. The entrepreneur had previously invested in online platforms such as Skype, Facebook, and Spotify, and he immediately saw the potential in Nick's app and was eager to invest in its development. Li Ka-Shing saw that Summly could be used for more than just summarizing webpages and web search information. Nick took up Li Ka-Shing's offer of an investment and started to develop his app further, expanding its capabilities.

Thanks to the hard work Nick put in, Summly continued to grow and attract the attention of the online world. This resulted in Yahoo! offering 18-year-old Nick around US $30 million for the rights to the app (Newstips, 2013). Nick took the deal and also signed on with Yahoo! as a product manager.

Akshay Ruparelia

Akshay Ruparelia is of Indian descent, although he was born in the United Kingdom, making him a first-generation British citizen. He spent most of his childhood in Harrow, London, after his parents fled India because of religious tensions. They placed a high value on education, and Akshay's mom is a teacher, which placed even more pressure on him to take his education seriously. Thankfully for his parents, Akshay worked hard in school, and got good grades. He was determined to make something out of himself, and so he spent his school breaks doing research into potential business ventures.

Soon his break-time brainstorming sessions moved on from being just idle daydreaming and took a more focused approach. Akshay narrowed his research down and began looking into just one of his many ideas; a business idea concerning disruptive tactics. This is where up-and-coming companies challenge established companies by concentrating on the unaddressed needs of the original companies' target market. Akshay wanted to create a real estate company that made moving more affordable for people. He had seen how his parents had struggled to pay all the extra costs that were added on when they bought a house. Akshay was sure there must be a way of reducing these costs. As his plans around his entrepreneurial venture became more solid, with business plans, website ideas, and company structures, Akshay gave the venture a name, Doorsteps.

In 2016, as Akshay was preparing to leave school, he received an offer to study economics and management at the University of Oxford. This was a great accomplishment and a fantastic opportunity. However, it also meant that if Akshay took the place offered to him by Oxford, he would have to put his plans for his entrepreneurial venture on hold.

Akshay chose the path taken less often and deferred his offer to Oxford, and focused all his attention on Doorsteps and the potential he saw in it. Akshay combined his desire to reduce the costs to house and land buyers with the company's integration of online and offline tools. This integration was done to attract buyers within the upper-income brackets.

Akshay had to take out a small loan as seed money, to get his company off the ground, but he was able to pay back the money very quickly. Within sixteen months of Doorstep's starting, it had become the 18th largest real estate company in the United Kingdom, selling around £100 million worth of property, and making its founder a millionaire.

Akshay's decision to defer his placement at Oxford paid off, as had all the hard work he had put in during those research sessions. His story shows us that one of the critical assets of being a successful entrepreneur is the ability to combine a willingness to take risks with well-thought out and researched plans.

Edward Shatverov

Edward Shatverov was born in 2001, in Los Angeles, California. His love for business and his entrepreneurial spirit were both clearly visible when he was growing up. Edward's entrepreneurial spirit was also spurred on by his desire to leave behind a legacy. He wanted to be remembered, not just by his loved ones but also by history.

As Edward grew, he became obsessed with marketing and investments. He spent a lot of his free time researching these generally. He looked at trends, and tried to understand how and why things happened in the markets. He also spent hours trying to unpick what was happening in the marketing industry.

The area of marketing and investments that Edward felt he understood the best – through his research was e-commerce. Before he spent any money though, he wanted to ensure that he understood it fully. He narrowed down his fields of research and began focusing only on marketing and investments that were directly related to e-commerce. He studied the trends and indicators that he felt had the greatest influence on the industry. Edward focused his research on the tactics of sites, such as Facebook and Instagram, observing their advertising methods. He also studied how email advertising worked and examined the strategy behind sales funnels. He spent his time seeing if he could accurately predict the outcome of potential investments and gauging his returns if he had put money in.

After countless hours of research, Edward felt he was ready to put some of his money on the line and to invest in those opportunities that he felt would give him the greatest return. Edward was just 15 years old when he took on this entrepreneurial risk. He began to invest his own money into different companies, and he saw returns almost immediately. His hours of research had paid off. The names of the companies that Edward had invested in remained a secret that he did not share; the young entrepreneur didn't want others to swoop in and grab the opportunities that he had spent years finding.

Edward's research and investment moves paid off and, by the time he was 18, he had become a millionaire. This made him one of those rare entities, a self-made teen millionaire. With this accomplishment in his pocket, the 18-year-old started to move away from simply investing in other people's e-commerce companies and began to create his own. Again, Edward chose to keep his direct ownership of these companies to himself. He wanted the companies to speak for themselves and not have their future dictated by his known involvement in them.

Despite Edward's secrecy concerning his business interests, he has a strong following on Instagram, where he shares inspirational content with young followers, urging them to take entrepreneurial risks. Edward is also working on creating an online course to teach others the skills he learned along his ow entrepreneurial journey. The key ideas he wants to share are for those interested in taking up self-employment. Some of his ideas are: stand out – find your niche, that thing that makes you different and use it to grow your business; look to future moves, you always need to be looking to the future and what you are going to do next; and finally, celebrate your results, good or bad because if they are bad you can see them as a learning point and can change them.

Chapter 3:
SALES/ MARKETING

Cameron Johnson

Cameron Johnson had a mind for business before most of us could do our multiplication tables correctly. He was just nine years old when he flexed his entrepreneurial muscles and started his first business.

Cameron's parents loved to throw parties for their friends. Cameron saw an opportunity in this, and he began creating invitations for his parents' parties. These invitations were not simple crayon drawings; in fact, they were so impressive that Cameron's parents and friends soon started to place orders with Cameron for invitations to their own parties, functions, and even simple cards for everyday use. Cameron named his budding business Cheers and Tears. His work was of such high quality, and his popularity so great, that by the time he was 11 years old he had managed to save up several thousand dollars. However, Cameron and his entrepreneurial skills were not finished; not by a long shot.

When Cameron turned 12 he saw the value in a seemingly silly and childish item, Ty Beanie Babies. He offered his sister $100 for her collection of fuzzy teddies. Little did his sister know he would make that $100 back in little to no time. In fact, he made ten times the amount he spent, by selling the collection on eBay. Inspired by his successful sale, Cameron soon began buying Ty Beanie Babies cheaply and reselling them to the right buyer for a substantial profit. In less than a year, Cameron had made himself $50,000 just by selling Ty Beanie Babies, and he was still not done. Instead of spending the money or letting it sit idle, he used it to help fund his next entrepreneurial adventure, My EZ Mail. My EZ Mail worked by forwarding emails to different accounts without taking the recipient's personal information from them. The emailing system quickly became popular and began generating Cameron $3,000 monthly (Forbes, 2009).

A true entrepreneur, he moved on to his next business adventure in 1997. This time Cameron brought in two of his friends, who were also young entrepreneurs, and they worked together to create an online advertising company, Surfingprizes.com. The company provided scrolling adverts that featured across the top of a user's browser. Anyone who downloaded the software was given 20 cents per hour for the inconvenience of having ads on their screens, but that was nowhere near what the boys were receiving from the companies advertising through them.

At 15 years old, Cameron's expertise as an entrepreneur was such that he was headhunted by a Tokyo-based company, which appointed him as a member of their board. In that year, Camron also released a book entitled "15-Year- old CEO" which became a fast best-seller. With all of his business success, book sales, and with 12 different companies to his name before the age of 18, it would be foolish for anyone to think that Cameron would not be a millionaire by the time he graduated from high school.

Henry McVey

Henry's first venture into the world of business was when he used the pocket money his dad had given him, while on a trip to Japan, to buy cool gadgets that he knew his friends would not have access to in the United Kingdom.

When he returned, he sold the gadgets to his friends at a 20% markup; Henry was just eight years old. Having gotten a taste for business, Henry's next entrepreneurial venture was the buying and selling of shares. Unfortunately, at the age of 12, Henry ran into some issues with his financial backer. Until then, his backer had been his dad. The problem was that Henry had been using his dad's credit card to fund his investments in stocks, without asking his dad's permission. Luckily for both Henry and his father, Henry had managed to invest the money he used in profitable shares. The two had a chat about the issue, and all was forgiven.

In 2000, when Henry was only 13 years old, he started his own import company, which soon made him a millionaire. Is there anything cooler than a micro scooter? Honestly, not really. Henry knew that and knew that if he could get a company to ship the scooters, he would have kids and teenagers chomping at the bit to buy them or – more likely – have their parents buy them for them. Henry's scooter business came about by accident. The young teen had meant to search the internet for information on Visa. However, he misspelled the word and searched for Viza, leading him to discover that the Viza was a micro "push-scooter", produced by a company in Arizona, in the United States. When Henry placed his first order with the company their sales department told him that if he bought five scooters from them, they would throw in an extra one for free. It is fair to say that Henry bought more than five from them, and soon he was getting a container a week shipped out. Overall he sold 11 million scooters.

With the sales of his scooters and his investments in shares, now made with his dad's approval, Henry became a millionaire long before leaving school. His parents worked with him, in his later teens, to help set some of his wealth aside in trust funds so that he would have a continued income, should any of his future entrepreneurial ventures 'go south'. They wanted to ensure that their son didn't lose any of his hard-earned money.

Alina Morse

Alina Morse lives with her parents and her little sister, Lola, in Michigan. The family is close-knit, and all of them have worked hard to help Alina along her entrepreneurial journey.

Alina's entrepreneurial spirit was evident almost from birth; when she was only three years old she announced to her family that when she grew up, she wanted to be a CEO. As soon as she could write, she began to write down all her different business ideas so she would not forget them. She then placed them all in her much-treasured ideas binder. In her binder were ideas for robot parents that could be used as doubles, so that parents could stay at home while they sent their doubles out to work; and tubs that combined peanut butter and jelly, thus making the preparation of PB&J sandwiches much easier.

When Alina was seven years old, she came up with the idea for Zollipops, sugar-free lollipops. She was at the bank with her dad and one of the tellers offered her a lollipop. Before Alina could take it, her dad said that she would rather not have it as she had eaten too much sugar lately and that it just might rot her teeth. This got Alina thinking about creating a delicious lollipop that would not cause her teeth to decay. She asked her dad if he could help her do some research on the internet. At first, her dad thought it was just another idea that Alina would write down and file away. It was not. Over the course of several months, she kept asking her father to help her. Eventually, he was so impressed by his daughter's determination that he decided he would help her. He showed her how to look up information, explained how to sort it out and then taught her to determine which information might be helpful and which was unnecessary.

Success with Alina's research didn't come quickly. It took her dad and her almost two years of online research – and unsuccessful experiments in the kitchen – before they found a recipe that worked well. To ensure that the lollipop recipe they came up with would not rot anyone's teeth, Alina asked her dad if they could check with a dentist and a food scientist to make sure that it was 'safe.'

Now that Alina had a recipe, which had the all-important approval of a dentist, she was ready to take the next step and start her very own company. Her three-year-old self, with her dreams of being a CEO, would have been over the moon. Alina took all of the money she had saved from past birthdays, Christmases, and holiday money and used it as the seed money for her company. In total, she had $3,750 (Akhtar, 2019). Her dad told her that he would also invest in her company by matching the total she had.

Alina called her company Zolli Candy with Zollipops being the company's main product, but it also produced other sugar-free, dentist-approved candies. At first, Alina and her family sold her Zollipops and other candies online; but, as the candies' popularity grew, Whole Foods Market began to sell the product in their stores. Zolli Candy made $70,000 in sales, and the company saw its sales double annually from 2014 through to 2018. Now, Zolli Candy can also be found in Krogers and on Amazon. In fact, Zollipops happens to be Amazon's best-selling lollipop. In 2019, Zolli Candy went global and is available in over 25,000 shops worldwide.

Alina understands how much her family helped and still help her with her business. Because of this, she asked her sister to work alongside her in the company. Her sister creates media content for Zolli Candy and is featured in most of their YouTube videos. Alina also made her sister a majority owner in the company in addition to herself, making the company one of the youngest woman-owned businesses. By the time Alina started high school, she had earned around $2.2 million from Zolli Candy. She plans to use some of her hard-earned money to fund her university studies, where she plans to study business and to use what she learns to strengthen her company and help it grow.

Leanna Archer

Leanna wants kids and teenagers to know that you are never too young to start something, all you need to have is passion and dedication. She wants young entrepreneurs to know that they must never let anything come between themselves and their dreams. Leanna's sentiments are more than just empty words; she has lived them out. When Leanna was only nine years old, she had her own line of hair products and she was the CEO of the company that made them; Leanna's Inc.

Leanna's journey to being the CEO of her own company started when she was seven, after her friends and teachers asked her – again and again – how she got her hair to look so healthy. Not having an answer, she asked her mom if she knew why. Her mom revealed that it was because she used Leanna's great-grandmother's many, secret, hair-treatment recipes. Empowered by this information Leanna realized that if she had the recipe, the ingredients, and some bottles, she would be able to share her great-grandmother's hair products with those who were always admiring her hair – for a price of course.

However, Leanna was a well-mannered child, and before she did anything with her idea, she wanted to get her parents' permission. Unfortunately for Leanna, her parents didn't share in her Leanna Archer entrepreneurial view, at least not then. They told their daughter that she was too young to do something like that, saying it would be best if she waited until she was in university, before she tried to start a business.

Leanna respected her mother, but didn't want to wait until she was older to start her business. Finally, her passion for her new idea won her mother over, and she got the go-ahead to start making and selling the products, using her great-grandmother's recipes. Leanna collected jars, with her brothers' help, rinsed them, and filled them with various products. She gave out small amounts of the product to her neighbors and friends to try, in an effort to get them interested and hoping they would pass on the news of her excellent product. In no time at all, Leanna began receiving orders for her mysteriously wonderful products, and people were willing to pay her far more than she had expected for them. Leanna's parents were completely in awe of their daughter's determination and the success of the products she was selling. They saw that they had been wrong not to believe that she could make something out of her idea and realized that they had misjudged her ability to be successful, because of her age. One year after Leanne started her business, her parents agreed to co-sign a business license with her, making Leanna's Inc an official company.

With her business doing well, Leanna wanted to give back to her community and her family. Therefore, in 2008, and at the age of 13 years old, she founded the Leanna Archer Education Foundation. This organization works to create opportunities for underprivileged children on the island country of Haiti.

At the age of 16, Leanna was the CEO of a business that had made her over $100,000 in revenue. Since then, her company has continued to grow, and her great-grandmother's hair products have helped thousands of people have lush, healthy hair (Steward '19, 2019).

Sean Belnick

Sean Belnick was always a business-minded kid. He started helping out around his neighborhood, offering his services as a gardener and mowing yards for a small fee. He then moved on to sales, using eBay to sell Pokémon cards. This was where he found his entrepreneurial gift as a salesman, which most probably came from observing his stepdad, who had been in the sales industry for over 20 years.

When Sean was 14, he came up with the concept of a drop-ship business model, which uses a third party to source and store products, and the original company ships the orders directly to the customer. Sean was fascinated by this sales concept; now, he just needed a product to sell, and the idea came from his stepdad. Sean used to hang out regularly at his stepdad's office-furniture store. One day, he realized that instead of customers coming to the store to look at and buy their products, he could set up a website that sourced the furniture for the customers, and then Sean could get the customers' purchases shipped directly to them. By creating an online marketplace for office furniture, Sean would be making life easier for the customers and would save his stepdad the cost of retail rent – that is, if he chose to join his stepson in his entrepreneurial adventure.

Sean put all of his ideas together, as well as the $500 he had in savings, and created BizChair.com. It took Sean a few weeks of research to learn how to create a website. He started the website, using a Yahoo! store account, as it proved to be the most cost-efficient means to transport the orders to his potential customer base. Before Sean let BizChair.com go live, he coordinated an advertising campaign to ensure that potential customers had heard about his new venture. Sean did all of his planning in the summer of 2001, and then BizChair.com went live with 100 different products for customers to choose between.

Sean began to receive his first orders, only a few hours after the launch!

BizChair.com grew quickly. This was okay while Sean was still on his summer holidays from school, but as the new school year approached, he knew he would not be able to keep up with the orders and still give school the time he needed. Realizing that Sean needed help, his stepdad offered his support. However, even with his step-dad's help, BizChair.com's growth meant that Sean still had to devote countless hours to the company, if he wanted to keep expanding his client base and the company's reach.

Sean's skills as a salesman and all his effort truly paid off; as his company grew and as it did, so did Sean's wealth. Upon leaving school, Sean had firmly cemented himself as a millionaire, and at 20 – six years after starting his company – Sean makes around $24 million in revenue a year, selling the furniture he sources to some rather big names; such as, the Pentagon, American Idol, Microsoft, and Google (Bluestein, 2020).

Tyler Dikman

Tyler Dikman was always thought of as an intelligent kid. He understood computers and technology in ways that most adults didn't. He also displayed an entrepreneurial flare from an early age, especially when it came to marketing, where he seemed able to make any service he offered irresistible to those around him.

Although it took a while for Tyler's skills in technology to become apparent, his marketing skills were obvious from as early as when he was five. When Tyler set up a small lemonade stand outside his house, he made sure that the whole community knew about his product, displaying adverts for his lemonade around the neighborhood. His effort paid off; he is thought to have made between £15 to £20 an hour from his lemonade sales. It either had to be some amazing lemonade or some genuinely inspiring adverts; or perhaps both. As Tyler grew older and became stronger and more responsible, he added lawn mowing and babysitting to his entrepreneurial CV.

When Tyler was thirteen, he used his skills in technology, combined with his entrepreneurial mindset, to start fixing computers for people in his neighborhood, charging £15 an hour. The service became a lot more popular than even Tyler had expected. This demonstrated to Tyler how in-demand his skills were, and out of that, he saw the potential for a fully-fledged company that catered to people's need for technological help.

At 15, Tyler created a business called CoolTronics. In its early days, CoolTronics only provided two services; repairs to people's computers and training for those who struggled with technology. In its early years, one of the company's biggest markets was grannies who needed help understanding how to use the internet. Tyler also worked hard to develop his own technological skills, broadening his coding and web development knowledge. With his new skills, Tyler was able to expand the services CoolTronics provided, as well as to market the existing services to a more professional client base. CoolTronics could now offer services, such as helping businesses make the most of their technological resources, offering clients in-depth training programs, and helping clients safeguard their computers against viruses. By 18, Tyler was providing salaried employment to a staff of ten and had made himself a millionaire.

Jonathan Koon

Jonathan Koon is a first-generation American from Queens, New York, whose parents immigrated to the USA from Hong Kong. From an early age onwards, Jonathan had a passion for cars, and he would spend hours looking through his dad's Japanese car magazines. He was obsessed with the super-sleek cars, most of which were custom-made. All Jonathan wanted was to be able to get one of the cars he had looked at in the magazines to Queens.

Jonathon's answer was born out of this longing. He could bring the car over or – if not the entire car – at least parts of it, which then be used to make his own custom cars, and exactly as he wanted them. Jonathan quickly realized that he could not be the only person, who wanted to be able to create their own custom car out of the high-quality Japanese parts that he had seen in his dad's car magazines.

He decided that he would take all of these entrepreneurial ideas and start a business from them. He named his company Extreme Performance Motorsports. Jonathon took the $5,000 he had saved up over the years, as his seed money, and he began to buy high-quality car parts from Japan. His business plan was to act as a middleman; that is he didn't sell the parts he imported directly to individual customers. Instead, he partnered with local mechanics and fabricators, eventually partnering with around 60 shops. They used the imported parts to soup up cars for their customers. Jonathon's partnership with the mechanics showed him that it was not only mechanical parts that were in demand but also good-quality finishers and audio systems.

Jonathan entered the world of car customization at the right moment, just as the idea of "pimped out" cars was becoming common. This shows Jonathan's entrepreneurial ability to see an opportunity before most people. Extreme Performance Motorsports went on to become the main parts' supplier for the TV program "Pimp my Ride."

At 16, and thanks to his hard work, Jonathan had become a millionaire.

Pierce Woodward

Pierce Woodward took a brave step towards being a self-made millionaire at the age of 16. Before he left school, he had been modeling part-time and realized that if he wanted to be successful at modeling, he would need to commit to it full-time, so with his parents' permission, he dropped out of school and began to work as a model. Luckily, he had already amassed a somewhat substantial Instagram following. He was by no means a fully-fledged social media influencer, but he was on the way towards becoming one.

Modeling was going reasonably well for Pierce, but he still hadn't achieved the level of wealth he wanted to. He realized that the only way he was going to be able to get the lifestyle he wanted would be to find another source of income. Unfortunately, this realization coincided with the rise of the COVID-19 pandemic. The pandemic not only made finding another suitable job harder, but it also impacted Pierce's ability to book modeling jobs.

Pierce was determined not to return to school to follow the same path as so many others. He did not want to give up on his plans to become a self-made millionaire. Then, one day he saw one of his friends creating hand-made rings, on a specially designed ring-shaping machine, and an idea struck him. Pierce went out and purchased a machine himself and began to work on making his own line of rings to sell. He very smartly chose to make his rings out of found metal spoons. This gave them a distinct look and lowered Pierce's expenses Pierce as did not have to buy metal to mold into rings.

Pierce needed to come up with a good marketing plan, if he wanted his rings to make a big enough impact to gain the amount of money he needed to live the lifestyle he dreamed of, so he drew on his experience in the modeling world. Pierce knew that he needed to market his product to the correct audience, to collaborate with influencers and brands, and to ensure that his rings had something unique about them that set them apart.

Pierce turned to TikTok to reach the target market he wanted, making videos of himself making his rings and advertising them, to let his audience know how best to order one. Thanks to the Instagram following he already had, Pierce's TikTok videos soon became popular as well. One of his videos was seen by Vinne Hacker, a content creator with a large following. VINNE shared Pierce TikTok video, and added hundreds of followers to Pierce's account, which brought in countless orders for rings. Vinne's sharing of Pierce's video also helped the young entrepreneur connect with other content creators, for collaborations Now creators and established brands were far more likely to partner with him.

As well as making a line of rings which customers can order, Pierce also customizes jewelry for his clients and those he collaborates with. He wants to be able to create pieces of jewelry that are authentic and which represent the individual for whom he is making them. This also helps to demonstrate to his target market that he values them and understands they all have individual tastes and preferences.

The risk Pierce took leaving high school paid off. He has become the self-made millionaire he always wanted to be, and he did it before he turned 18. Now, he is able to now fund that luxury lifestyle he always wanted.

Chapter 4:

FOOD

Cory Nieves

Cory Nieves didn't come from money. The son of a single mom; he quickly learned the value of money, because it was something that his mom and he didn't have. What Cory did have, however, was determination; something he most likely got from his mom. Cory was born to Lisa Howard, when she was just 16 years old, and although money was tight, Lisa made sure that her baby son was well cared for and she did all she could to make sure he was a healthy and happy kid.

In the winter of 2009, Cory and his mom moved from the Bronx to suburban New York. Unfortunately, the family didn't have a car, and public transport was not as regular in the suburbs as it was in the Bronx, which meant that Cory and his mom often found themselves outside in the cold waiting for the bus. During these cold moments of waiting, six-year-old Cory dreamed of having a nice comfortable car in which his mom could drive him around. He decided that he would take this dream and make it a reality. He had already learned from his mom that working hard was the best way to get those things you needed or wanted. He decided to make the family car a reality by selling hot cocoa and cookies at their local pizza place.

Cory got some help from his mom and began his business. The homemade cookies proved to be more popular than the cocoa, and Cory began selling his products at the local farmer's markets in the area, rather than the pizza place. The business grew slowly but steadily, and Cory's dream of affording a car seemed to be developing well. Unfortunately, in 2012, someone reported Cory to the local health department for food-safety violations. The department stated that if Cory wanted to stay in business, he said that he would have to make his cookies in a commercial kitchen.

Luckily, a good Samaritan heard about Cory's problem and offered the young entrepreneur the use of his kitchen, which was up to code. Now in a suitable location, Cory continued to work towards his dream car.

In 2014, Cory's business, now called Mr. Cory's Cookies, got its big break, when ABC News Huffington heard about Cory's company and his ambition to buy a car for his family. The subsequent articles secured Cory and his mom an invitation to the Ellen DeGeneres show. Ellen was so taken by Cory and his desire to work hard and dream big that she surprised him with a donation of $10,000 as well as a car customized with his business logo. these gifts meant that Cory could pour all of the money he had been saving for a car into his business, adding more capital to grow the business. Cory also continued to use the media attention to his advantage. Mr. Cory's Cookies can now be ordered and hand-delivered in central and northern New Jersey, plus all five boroughs. Cory has his dream car as well as $1,000,000 in the bank, and all before graduating high school.

FARR-OUT FOODS

Farrah Gray

Farrah Gray didn't have an easy beginning in life; he was one of five children born to a single mom. His dad left the family when Farrah was still very young, and his mom raised her kids in a crumbling apartment block in the projects of Chicago's south side.

However, Farrah was a determined young boy, who was set on making something of himself. This determination first showed itself when Farrah was only six years old. He started his entrepreneurial career by selling homemade creams and hand-painted rockets door-to-door in his community. Farrah's determination manifested itself in self-confidence. At seven years old, he made sure he always had a copy of his own 'professional' business cards which read "21st Century CEO."

When Farrah was eight, he realized that not everyone in his community had the determination and vision he had. Therefore, he and some others in his community founded the Urban Neighborhood Enterprise Economic Club (U.N.E.E.C.) on Chicago's southside, as a means of uplifting kids who didn't know how they could lift themselves up as Farrah was trying to do.

At a surprisingly young age, and when most kids are obsessed with cartoons, Farrah understood that if you wanted to be successful, you needed to educate yourself. He realized that the best way to succeed at something was to understand it as fully as possible; you needed to do the research, practice, and study. Farrah knew that, if you did not do these things, you would enter into your entrepreneurship with your eyes closed and probably fail before you had truly started.

When Farrah was thirteen, he founded Farr-out Foods, a company that made specialty food items and sold them throughout New York City. The company was an instant success; by the time Farrah turned 14, orders for Farr-out Foods had made over $1.5 million (Ndegwa, 2017).

This success allowed Farrah to open up his own office on Wall Street and to transform U.N.E.E.C. The organization became what is now New Early Entrepreneur Wonders, focusing on at-risk youth, and helping to educate those in its programs. It empowers them with the tools needed to set up their own businesses and prevents them from turning to illegal means of income generation.

Farrah's success with Farr-out Foods also meant he could found several other businesses; such as, KIDS TEL prepaid phone cards, the One Stop Mail Boxes, and The Teenscope's "Youth AM/FM." Teenscope's "Youth AM/FM" was a stepping stone to Farrah's reaching 12 million people on "Backstage Live," a Saturday night TV and radio show that he co-hosted.

Farrah made himself a multimillionaire before the age of 18, through his determination and ability to grab every opportunity presented to him. Farrah understands that – most often – success is not something that happens overnight or by accident. He also understands that – in order to be a truly successful person – you cannot go it alone. You need to have a community of people around you, helping you along and picking you up when you make a mistake.

Mikaila Ulmer

If you looked at Mikaila's Ulmer's resumé, you would find an impressive list of accomplishments; founding a company, receiving a $60,000 investment from Daymond John, having your product sold by Whole Foods, appearing on "Good Morning America" and NBC News, and having articles written about you by Forbes and Time magazines

(Bach, 2017). Add being recognized by the National Retail Foundation, speaking at the WE Day Seattle conference, and introducing the then-president Barack Obama and it sounds like a list of accomplishments from someone well into their adult life. However, Mikaila Ulmer was not an adult when she made these accomplishments; in fact, she had not yet had her 13th birthday.

The catalyst that led Mikaila to accomplish so much seems almost silly, and something most kids would forget about within a few weeks. When Mikaila was four, she was stung by a bee, twice in one week. At first, these stings made Mikaila extremely scared of bees. However, her parents did not want their daughter to form a lifelong fear of the little creatures, so they began to teach her as much as they could about them, even encouraging Mikaila to do her own research. The young girl soon discovered that bees are endangered and that their falling numbers could have terrible consequences for the planet.

Mikaila was moved by the sad reality that faced bees and wanted to do something to help them. She decided she would start selling lemonade. Luckily for her, she and her family had a fantastic flaxseed lemonade recipe that had been passed down to them from Mikaila's great-grandmother. Mikaila began to make the lemonade and sold it to various people around her neighborhood, even supplying a local pizza place. She named her new business Me & the Bees Lemonade and ten percent of her profits went to a local organization, dedicated to protecting honey bees (Bach, 2017). Mikaila's lemonade grew in popularity, and her parents thought it would be an excellent opportunity for her to have a stall, selling it, at the Acton Children's Business Fair and Austin Lemonade Day. To give her lemonade a fun twist and to promote the idea of saving the bees, the lemonade Makaila sold at these two events was slightly different from her previous lemonade. Instead of using sugar as a sweetener, she replaced it with honey.

The new lemonade recipe was a smash hit, with orders for the product coming in thick and fast. Mikaila sought support from outside investors to get enough capital to support the increased demand and to ensure that it continued to grow. She appeared on ABC's Shark Tank and got a $60,000 investment from Daymond John, giving him a 25% share of the company (Shark Tank Blog, 2015). The investment was just what Mikaila and Me & the Bees Lemonade needed. Soon the lemonade was being stocked in more than 500 stores across the United States, and Mikaila had made herself a millionaire; one who continues to fight for the protection of the honey bee.

Unfortunately, she is a millionaire who still has to attend school, which she admits can sometimes be challenging. Having to choose between a TV appearance and a math test can be tricky. Despite this fact, Mikaila continues to work hard both at school and in her business.

Fraser Doherty

At 18 years old, Fraser Doherty became the United Kingdoms' youngest-ever self-made millionaire. Even more impressive is that Fraser did it by making and selling a product that, while quintessentially British, is generally associated with grandmothers and not teenage boys.

Fraser made his millions by selling homemade jam, which he started making out of his parent's kitchen.

When Fraser was 14 years old, he wanted to make himself a little extra spending money, as we all do. His grandmother had a fantastic jam recipe that everyone always raved about. Fraser saw an entrepreneurial opportunity in the jam's popularity and began to make it in his parent's kitchen, and then bottling and selling it. Although the jam was good and sold well, Fraser wanted to give his product a special edge, so he worked on the recipe, tweaking it here and there. Eventually he came up with a way of making it 100% from fruit. Fraser called the new fruit jam SuperJam and that also became the name of his company.

Fraser decided to take a big step and present his product to the major supermarket chain, Waitrose, on the off chance that the supermarket would want to stock it. Well, Waitrose was very impressed by Fraser and his products, although they felt that it needed a little bit more polish before they could stock it in their stores. Fraser went away and worked to improve his product's look, making it fit the Waitrose target market better.

When Fraser returned to Waitrose with his redesigned look for SuperJam, a year later, they agreed to stock the product in their stores. Thanks to Fraser's deal with Waitrose, his entrepreneurial talents became known across the country. At 17, he was invited to a dinner at Downing Street with 20 others, to discuss how best to promote young entrepreneurship in the United Kingdom.

Following the Waitrose deal, other supermarkets showed interest in Fraser's product, including Tesco, Asda, and Morrisons, and all agreed to stock and sell the jam. SuperJam's popularity continued to grow, and it is now sold in Japan and South Korea. Although the product Fraser decided to sell might have seemed to some like a bit of an odd choice for boy, he was able to see the possibility it contained. He also worked hard to ensure that his product was marketable, and he made the changes that needed to be made, to ensure it would be a success and that he would become a millionaire.

Jack Bonneau

I n 2014, an eight-year-old wanted a Lego set, which was way too expensive for him to finance on his own—or so he thought. His dad and he set up lemonade stands throughout that summer and came up with much more than what the Lego set cost. In 2016, ABC's *Shark Tank* featured a 10-year-old Jack Bonneau, who wanted $50,000 in return for a 10% equity in his lemonade stall and other marketplace startup businesses. His pitch heavily relied on how his venture would help kids like him learn the basics of business, logistics, and profits by setting up marketplace stands.

In fact, Jack's presence on *Shark Tank* had been one of those momentous coincidences one might dream of. He was in New York for *The Today Show* when he heard of an open audition for *Shark Tank* in Manhattan. *Carpe diem*-like, he seized the opportunity which presented itself before him with both hands and made the most of it. He made himself available early enough to make the line and bravely made his pitch all on his own. He says even today that his biggest *win* had been in presenting his ideas to the Sharks and that every other outcome of it was *icing on the cake*. Though the Sharks were impressed by his acute entrepreneurial abilities and business acumen, they thought him too green a hand at the time. A few weeks later, Jack was called and told that his pitch had been accepted on one condition. One of the guest-Sharks offered him a loan for the amount he sought, at a two percent interest rate, which he accepted. After several video submissions and a ton load of paperwork later, Jack was signed on. The rest, as they say, was history. Only, Jack continues to make history even today!

Jack set up two companies: Jack's Stands & Marketplaces and Teen Hustl; fun avenues for kids to develop financial literacy and an idea of how businesses operated as they made money off them. Jack's Stands & Marketplaces gave kids the opportunity to put up their stalls and stands at places such as farmers' markets, malls, and other events in Colorado. Jack would buy products at wholesale rates and then sell them at retail rates. The stall operators would get to keep all the tips in addition to 8-10% of every item sold. Kids could also register to put up their own stalls as part of the venture.

Teen Hustl employs teenagers as delivery agents for food and other items picked up from local grocery stores and restaurants. The agents also deliver Amazon and other courier parcels on weekends and when customers are home, saving them from porch thefts. Moreover, Teen Hustlers pick up parcels that customers would like to return via Amazon or other online stores. Each agent is provided an electric scooter, LED-lit helmets, and GoPro cameras for parcel integrity; for their own and the customer's safety. Jack keeps tweaking his business models and nipping problems in the bud as they appear. For this little CEO, work is always in progress.

Apart from his companies, Jack is a motivational speaker who has used platforms such as TEDx, CBS, and local school events to speak to the youths who want to learn more about commerce and integrate that learning with essential social skills. He often talks about how kids could become their own best role models if they followed their passion, gut instincts, and the urge to just go ahead and do it. He has also spoken about the crucial need for inculcating entrepreneurial skills among high schoolers and teenagers across schools in the country so that they become more confident as they learn real-world skills and increase business awareness and financial skills.

When in an interview, Jack was asked about the biggest lessons he had learned, he revealed the three mantras that got him where he was. His entire journey sums up his ideals, *it's okay to fail, be curious, and look for help*, and *it's worth it* (*"It's Worth It" and Other Words of Advice from a 12-Year-Old Lemonade Tycoon*, 2019).

Chapter 5:

ENTERTAINMENT

Evan of YouTube

When Evan was just eight years old, he came up to his dad with a fun activity they could do together. Like most kids born in the mid-2000s, Evan had grown up watching YouTube videos every day. He wanted to see if he could make some videos of his own. Evan didn't want to do anything serious; he just wanted to create videos filled with all the many different activities he enjoyed doing.

Evan's first video was uploaded on September 21, 2011. It was a 30-second, stop-motion clip made with some of Evan's Angry bird plushies. Evan's channel, called, mainly showed the viewers the various toys and fun snacks he had been given. Evan's channel started with a modest following of only a few hundred views a week. However, as his channel became more popular, he gained the viewership of kids around his age and their parents, and some toy companies reached out to Evan and his dad. They pitched the idea of Evan doing 'unboxing videos', a popular trend on YouTube that involves creators unpacking different products and giving viewers their reviews of them. One of the biggest brands that Evan unboxes is Lego. Although Evan was not the first YouTube creator to do unboxing videos, his unboxing videos quickly became one the most popular in the genre and on his channel.

Five years after starting his channel and uploading his first video, Evan's channel hit 1.7 billion views in January of 2016, a truly groundbreaking number. Evan and his dad attribute his success to Evan's consistency. He uploads content regularly and is not overly disheartened when a video gets low viewing numbers. Rather, he works on finding out why the viewership was down and works to adapt his videos so that when he uploads again he is better able to reach out to his target ordinance. As Evan's popularity has grown, he has also collaborated with other well-known YouTubers, and appears on different channels on the platform, such as AnimalBytesTV.

Like any child, Evan develops, and as he does his interests broaden. As Evan entered his teenage years, he grew interested in gaming. As before, Evan wanted to share his interest with his viewers. To do this, he created a new channel called EvanTubeGaming and began uploading game reviews and clips of him playing in 2013. On this channel, Evan tends to record himself reviewing and playing popular games, but he also focuses on those he finds the most entertaining and fun to play, such as Fortnite and Minecraft.

Evan started out as a rather quiet, private person, who shared a little of his personal life with views, mainly because he was only six when he started his YouTube journey. As he has grown up, he has also begun to share more of his day-to-day life with viewers, or at least those parts he thinks his viewers will find interesting. Evan does this through his vlog, on his channel EvanTubeRaw. (A vlog is a visual diary of a person's life or part of their life.) EvanTubeRaw has since become The Tube Family, as now it shares not only Evan's life but also that of his whole family.

Evan started his YouTube channel as something fun to do with his dad and not as an entrepreneurial venture. Nevertheless, he has grown it into a thriving multi-million dollar business, where his top-grossing channel is EvanTubeGaming, which makes him over a million dollars annually. He has worked hard to make sure that the content he produces is relevant and fun, and he has adapted and changed the content he creates to make sure he remains popular.

Donald Dougher

Donald Dougher is a sixteen-year-old living in Los Angeles, California with his parents and older sister.

Like the majority of the kids born in the mid-2000s, Donald grew up seeing the impact of YouTube on the world of celebrities. He was a witness to the creation of internet influencers; people who became famous through their presence on social media rather than through movies, books, TV shows, inventions, or political actions. Inspired by the social media influencers he grew up with, Donald set out to become one of them. He spent years learning from simply watching their rises and falls and he felt confident that he would be able to triumph himself.

Donald started his online journey toward influencer status in 2019, with the launch of his YouTube channel called, DonLad. He also set himself up on Instagram and TikTok, to ensure he reached as broad an audience as possible. He created the hashtag #Ladiators to make it simpler for his followers to find his content on any social media platform.

Donald's content mainly focuses on lifestyle vlogging; he takes his followers around with him as he goes about his day-to-day life in Los Angeles. Having said that, some of what he does seems to have been planned out in advance and rather extravagant for the normal day-to-day life of a teen. Donald also makes prank videos for his channel, where he pranks his friends and family. He learned from the influencers before him that collaborating with other influencers is an excellent way to grow your following. These collaborations make it possible for Donald to reach out to a target market that is not yet following him. In the past, he has collaborated with other influencers and YouTubers such as Tanner Fox, Piper Rockelle, FaZe Rug, Sawyer Sharbino, Brawadis, and Funk Bros.

Donald has created a particular image for himself; he comes across as very boisterous and swaggering. He has self-titled himself as the "Richest Kid in America." Luckily for him, although this title is not true, his YouTube channel has made him a millionaire; he is worth close to $1.2 million. In his videos, he showcases a lavish lifestyle filled with expensive cars, a vast mansion, and name-brand clothing items. He has also added to his wealth through advertising and sponsorships, on all of his social media platforms, especially Instagram where he has a big following. Donald has also created his own clothing line under the name Fat Cat by Donald, which he aims specifically at his target market.

Despite his on-camera persona Donald is said to be a pretty typical teenager. He enjoys playing tennis and playing on his school's tennis team, and he loves getting takeout with his family, his favorite being sushi.

What Donald has been able to do, as a young entrepreneur, is to examine the careers of those influencers who came before him and build on the groundwork they laid. He improved on areas where they may have made mistakes or not taken full advantage of the situation. Donald also understands that you need to be well-branded when you become an entrepreneur, building your business around social media. He knows that self-marketing is vital in the world of social media influencers and entrepreneurs, where you need to create an identity around yourself that allows people to recognize you immediately.

Isabella Barrett

sabella Barret comes from Rhode Island, New England. She was born on August 8th, 2006, and grew up with her parents and older sister, Victoria.

When Victoria was younger, she faced many bullying issues at school, so a counselor recommended to the girl's mother that Victoria try participating in the local beauty pageants, in the hope of growing her confidence. Aged four, Isabella tagged along with her mom and sister and soon fell in love with the event and everything that came with it. The advice to enter Victoria into the local beauty pageants ended up being not only helpful for Victoria – as it did help her with her confidence – but it also changed the life trajectory of her sister, Isabella.

Victoria soon grew out of the need or desire to participate in pageants, but Isabella loved them, and her mom continued to let her join in. She participated in countless pageants, winning 85 titles and 55 different crowns. The biggest pageant that she won was Little Miss America in 2012, and she was just six years old when she won the title. Like many other successful pageants contestants of this time, Isabella also appeared several times on TLC's reality show Toddlers & Tiaras.

Similar to her sister, although Isabella enjoyed her time on the show and doing the pageants, she no longer felt the pull toward them as she grew older. However, she did enjoy the wealth she had accumulated from participating in all of it. Isabella's parents helped her manage her money, putting the majority of it aside for when she was older and giving her a hefty allowance each month.

Isabella took some of that saved pocket money and set herself up as a social media influencer. She already had a substantial online following, thanks to her time in the pageant scene. She created a YouTube channel named after herself, which currently has around 22,000 followers. On it, she focuses mainly on documenting her life through vlogs and uploads makeup and hair tutorials. She also has a strong presence on Instagram, with 56,000 followers, and 1,200 on Twitter.

Once Isabella had established herself a little more securely on social media, she launched a clothing and jewelry line called Glitzy Girl. She also took up modeling, and – most notably – appeared on the runways of New York Fashion Week. She also created a music group called LOL with Eden Woods, a close friend that she made during her time doing pageants. Isabella has also released several songs on her own. All of Isabella's different social media platforms, projects, and businesses have made her a multi-millionaire several times over.

Isabella's fame may have come first through somewhat traditional means – a TV show – however she has taken that fame and created something all her own. She has worked hard to become a successful social media influencer and entrepreneur, even though she has yet to turn 18. She took what was given to her and multiplied it, demonstrating that even though you can sometimes stumble into fame, it takes hard work to turn that fame into real success.

Mia Talerico

Mia Talerico was born in Santa Barbara California, and grew up with her mom, dad, and younger sister, Aubrey. She was a bundle of energy and had a personality that could charm just about anyone. Seeing her potential, Mia's parents allowed her to appear in adverts and short clips. Renowned producers, Phill Baker and Drew Vaupen, saw some of Mia's clips and they also saw a future talent in her. They wanted her charm for their upcoming Disney show; so, in 2011 the producers called her up, and she landed a lead role in Good Luck Charlie. At just three years old, she had to begin to learn how to memorize lines and work with co-workers who were often far more than triple her age. These potential issues didn't faze Mia; in fact, she thrived in the environment.

The show was an insistent hit because Mia's character, Charlie, was incredibly loveable, and Mia captured the personality and the nature of the character perfectly. People were drawn to her different antics and shared them on social media. The most famous, of which a GIF was made, was of her shrugging her shoulders in confusion. Her performance as Charlie was nominated for a Kids Choice award in 2014.

Towards the end of Good Luck Charlie's run on the Disney Channel, Mia's social media accounts, which were then run by her parents, received messages that threatened violence towards the young actor. These messages caused Mia's parents to withdraw her from the public eye, and they limited the information they posted about her as well as her public appearances for the show. This exile ended the threatening messages and gave Mia the opportunity to experience a 'normal' life without the pressure of celebrity. She enjoys crocheting, but also loves to be outside enjoying activities such as hiking and surfing.

As she grew older, Mia took over the running of her social media accounts, from her mom. She started to post more about her day-to-day life on her Instagram, sharing her fashion insights and talking about the fun activities she does with her sister and friends. She also has two TikTok accounts. One is her personal account where she shares fun moments from her life and participates in the popular dance trends on the site. Her other account is for her pet guinea pig, where Mia shares this little creature's cuteness with the rest of the world. Mia's fans from her time on Good Luck Charlie have followed her into the world of social media, and she is fast on her way to establishing herself as a fully-fledged influencer. What is lucky for her is that she has the money to fund the lifestyle needed to be an influencer. Her time working on Good Luck Charlie securely cemented her as a millionaire.

Syed Sumail Hassan

Syed Sumail Hassan was born in Pakistan in 1999, and lived there until he was 13, with his parents and older brother Yawar Hassan. Both the boys loved gaming and played a variety of games. When Syed was eight years old, they began to play Dota, a fantasy multiplayer online battle arena. When he was 13, his family immigrated to the United States, settling in Chicago, Illinois. The move was a significant change for the family, as they went from living a relatively comfortable life in Pakistan to living on a very tight budget in a small apartment in the city. The one significant upside for Syed was that their family's internet connection was much better than the one they had had in Pakistan, and having a faster internet meant that there was no time lag when he and his brother played Dota2, so Syed was able to play more regularly.

With the extra time that he was able to spend playing, his skill at the game strengthened. Syed decided to out the extra practice and the skills he had built up during years of playing to good use and to compete in the American Elite League. He was a smash hit. He rose through the game's ranks and quickly became the League's highest-rated player. Syed's meteoric rise in the Dota2 league caught the attention of Evil Geniuses, an American e-sports organization. Their top player, Saahil Arora, was amazed by Syed's abilities and urged Evil Geniuses to sign him as one of their players. Syed accepted Evil Geniuses' offer and joined them in 2015.

Evil Geniuses were not disappointed with their signing, as Syed proved to be an instrumental player in the team, which took third place in the Asia Championships group stage. He then carried on proving his worth, by helping them as they progressed past the group stage. Syed and the team were victorious at the event, thanks largely to the amazing efforts of Syed. In his last game alone he was able to achieve 17 kills, seven deaths, and 11 assists. Evil Geniuses' win meant that Syed became the youngest player – at 16 – to win a Vale-sponsored event, and he won a share of the $1,200,00 event prize money (Bonifacio, 2020).

Syed's popularity in the world of gaming keep growing and he continued to compete for Evil Geniuses, as well as playing Dota2 on his own. He also continued to bring in money for his family by winning competitions and sponsorship deals. Syed and his family were soon able to move out of the apartment they had moved into in 2012, as he became a millionaire. Syed used the skills, so often looked down upon by adults as childish and silly, to lift his family up and to give them a more secure future.

In 2016, he was named one of Time magazine's 30 Most Influential Teens of the year. In 2019, he moved from Evil Geniuses to play for Quincy Crew. What was nice was that being on Quincy Crew meant that he got to play on the same team as his brother. In 2020 he moved to join the team OG, and today he plays for Nigma Galaxy.

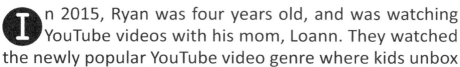

Ryan Kaji

In 2015, Ryan was four years old, and was watching YouTube videos with his mom, Loann. They watched the newly popular YouTube video genre where kids unbox and review different toys. Ryan absolutely loved the videos; they totally enthralled him. He had one minor concern; why didn't he have his own YouTube channel?

He kept on mentioning this to his mom, about how much he wanted his own channel and how much fun it would be. Eventually, his mom gave in, and the pair started working together to create the channel Ryan's ToysReview. The very first few months after the channel went live brought in very few views, but this didn't actually worry four-year-old Ryan, who just enjoyed making the videos with his mom. However, about four months into the channel's life, Ryan and his mom filmed and uploaded a video entitled: GIANT Lightning McQueen Egg Surprise with 100+ Disney Cars Toys. The video was an instant hit, and the views of the channel began to grow exponentially and it eventually gained over two billion views. The channel was getting so many views that Ryan's mom was finding it hard to cope with the channel as well as her high school chemistry teacher's job. She decided to grab onto her son's enthusiasm, take a leap of faith, and quit her job, dedicating all her work hours to Ryan ToysReview .

For the next four or so months, Ryan ToysReview became the most popular YouTube channel in the United States and the second most popular in the world. This popularity made the channel a household name, alongside people like Justin Bieber or websites such as Buzzfeed, which was at its international peak at that time. The site's popularity meant that Ryan's videos brought in $1 million a month from the advertising on the videos alone. This was not taking into account the sponsorship and partnership deals they gained from companies who wanted to get in on the popularity of Ryan ToysReview . In 2017, Ryan's channel made him the eighth highest-paid YouTuber in the world, and in 2019 he made it to the top of the list by earning $26 million. Ryan and his mom also added to the money Ryan made by parenting with Pocket.watch to launch a line of toys inspired and partly designed by Ryan. The toys were available at 75 physical locations upon their launch and are available to order online.

Despite Ryan's young age, he does not leave all of the hard work to his mom, and works hard to grow his entrepreneurial spirit and skills. He does his own research by watching fellow YouTubers, who are also doing unboxing and toy reviews. Observing these other YouTubers helps Ryan see what he could do better and how those in his field interact with their audiences. His favorites to watch are EvanTubeHD and Hulyan Maya. Ryan and his mom try to release one video a day, which helps to keep their views consistent. They also added some vlog-style videos to the channel, as they became more popular. The channel changed its name from Ryan ToysReview to Ryan's World, after they added the vlog-style videos, as they felt the title better suited the channel's new style.

Ryan has just started to spread his wings in the entrepreneurial world. He helps his mom, especially in the creative parts of the channel, and he is starting to do market research. However, he cannot take on all the complex, complicated decisions that go into the day-to-day running of the business he and his mom have made together, yet. After all he is only 11 years old.

Truth Jones

If you asked most kids whether they enjoy writing 500 word essays for English, they will probably answer no. Then, if you asked them if they wanted to spend most of their spare time writing an entire book, you would probably be laughed at. However, if you had asked Truth Jones these questions, you would have gotten a very different answer; mainly because Truth has already written and published his first book.

Growing up, Truth experienced quite a bit of negativity and bullying, which profoundly impacted him. Ever since he was a small child, Truth had felt a pull towards American Football. He loved to watch the game, but even more, he loved to play it. Unfortunately, when Truth was seven years old, he had some horrible interactions with his teammates, who bullied him. When he turned to his coach for help, he was met with indifference rather than support. Additionally, because he didn't mix well with the other boys on the team, his coach saw him as a bench player who brought little or no value to the team. Truth was devastated. He needed to find a way to deal with all of the pain that came with having something so close to his heart turn into a nightmare.

Thankfully, Truth was not alone. His mom was a source of comfort to him, always there to lift her son up and to remind him of his worth. Truth also had his Christian faith which played a key role in his identity and his ability to cope with his feelings. Truth's mom encouraged her son to write down his feelings and frustrations. Truth did just this; he wrote down all the hard feelings he had had to deal with and, gradually, he began to see how those feelings could be overcome with a positive and proactive attitude.

Truth's mom was blown away by her son's writing, and she encouraged him to transform his feelings into a story form, creating a book. Truth did just this, writing a book under the title: The Win Within. Truth explained that the book focuses on three main points: Faith, family, and football. The book tells Truth's story about his ability to overcome and to learn to trust in God.

Truth's mom was determined to get Truth's story out there, so that it could help other kids who were struggling with similar issues; so, when Truth was eight and with his mom's help, his book was published. In the first 90 days, Truth and his mom sold 500 copies, and as sales increased word of mouth about the book increased. Soon, Truth was getting calls from schools and youth groups, asking him to give talks and to share his story with kids and adults alike.

As money began to come in from his book sales, Truth used it to help start-ups and investment portfolios. The now 14-year-old Truth started to invest his money in the stock market. He was a natural at it. He seemed to be able to see just the right stocks to buy and when to sell them. Truth's newfound skills on the stock market, coupled with his book sales and speaking events, lifted Truth into the income bracket of a millionaire, just as he was leaving middle school.

Truth is an example of what can happen when you take something bad that has happened to you and look at it from an optimistic viewpoint. Truth used his pain to enrich his life, personally, spiritually, and financially. He then took the 'blessings' he received from putting his story out into the world and made a better, more stable life for himself and his mom, by embracing the risks of the entrepreneurial world.

Vlad and Niki

Vladislav and Nikita, known as Vlad and Niki, are brothers who live in Miami, Florida, with their parents. They are Russian-American, as both of their parents immigrated to the United States, from Moscow, Russia, before the boys were born.

Vlad and Niki asked their parents if they could start making their own videos for YouTube, after watching other young kids on the platform. They didn't want to do toy reviews or unboxing videos like many other young YouTubers were doing. They wanted to have a channel that documented their fun and creative playtime. Their channel, which went live in 2018, is basically what would happen if someone created a sitcom about a preschool. The channel is simply called Vlad and Niki. The boys' ability to speak both English and Russian means that they can upload some videos for Russian-speaking audiences.

The boy's channel was an instant hit, with subscriptions and views being added after each upload. As of 2021, the boy's channel had 81 million global subscribers, and collectively they had 99 billion views on all of their videos. These fantastic statistics made the boys the ninth most-watched YouTube channel in the world. That year (2019) continued to be a good year for the boys and they won several prestigious awards in the world of social media; including the Best Web Series for Kids, and the Best Influencers & Celebrity YouTube Campaign. They were also the Bronze Winners in the General Children's Online category.

Because Vlad and Niki made videos in Russian and English, their parents thought it would be a draw if kids who spoke other languages were able to watch and enjoy the boys' fun antics. Consequently, their videos have been translated and dubbed. Today, they are available in German, Spanish, French, Portuguese, Hindi, and Arabic.

In 2019, Haven Global partnered with the boys and their parents to develop new content. Vlad and Niki's success and their YouTube channel have made them multi-millionaires. It is calculated that the boys make around $30 million a year from their YouTube channel and then close to $200 million from sponsorships deals and branded toys and clothing (De Luce & Gray, 2021).

Vlad and Niki are only at the beginning of their entrepreneurial journey. They have a lot of creativity and inspiration, but they still need a little help from mom and dad regarding the day-to-day running of their business.

Anastasia Radzinskaya

Anastasia Sergeyevna Radzinskaya was born on January 27, 2014, in Krasnodar Krai, Russia. She now lives in the United States, in Florida, with her parents. When Anastasia was born, there was much concern about her health. She was diagnosed with cerebral palsy, which is a disorder – with varying levels of severity – that affects a person's ability to move and maintain their balance. Although Anastasia had a less severe level of the condition, it still impacted her health at birth. The doctors were also unsure if Anastasia would be able to talk when she was older. To help them cope, and to improve awareness of the condition, Anastasia's parents started to vlog, uploading videos on YouTube about their expenses, treatment, and the new normal of their lives.

As Anastasia's parents became more familiar with her condition and how best to help her deal with it, they posted less and less, but they didn't stop altogether. As Anastasia grew older, her mom began to capture sweet moments and activities between the little girl and her dad. Some of the videos they posted were just Anastasia's playing her made-up fantasy games, but the couple soon noticed that these videos got more views than the others.

By 2014, kids and families on YouTube were nothing out of the ordinary and young content creators were often the most popular creators on the website. Anastasia's parents could see that their daughter and her activities were making their videos popular; however, they didn't just want to use Anastasia for content. If she was to become popular on YouTube, it would have to be her choice. The channel would ultimately have to be hers, and in that way she could assume more control of running it, as she grew older. The YouTube channel was named Like Nastya and Anastasia became its full-time star.

Like Nastya still has family vlog videos uploaded to it regularly. However, most of the content is now short comedy skits, lessons on responsibility, and games, mainly between Anastasia and her dad. Anastasia's parents have to be highly careful when they create the videos they upload and Anastasia needs to have her own creative input into the videos.

The family's willingness to be vulnerable and to share their struggles around Anastasia's birth as well as involving her and making her a part of the creative process has paid off. The pint-size creator has been able to capture the attention of a younger target group on YouTube. Most of the viewers watching her videos are around her age. Kids love seeing other kids and the normal everyday things they do in the videos they watch. Watching According to Forbes, Anastasia's channel made her one of the wealthiest YouTubers of 2021, and established her as a multi-millionaire before she was even ten years old.

Jacob Sartorius

Imagine posting a couple of lip-syncing videos on your social media handle for fun and then learning that you have become an internet star almost overnight. Well, that's pretty much what happened to Jacob Sartorius. He posted his videos on Musical.ly, the precursor to TikTok, and became a sensation. He then capitalized on his fame and went on to become a singer in his own right and released his first single, "Sweatshirt", in 2016, which was listed on the Hot 100 in the USA and Canada.

Rolf Jacob Sartorius, born in Oklahoma, was put up for adoption by his birth parents and grew up with his adoptive parents in Virginia. His love for performing began with his acting in musicals as early as when he was seven. By a little later than mid-2016, he had over eight million followers on Vine, a short video hosting platform, which ceased operations a couple of months later. Jacob says he had begun using social media as an escape from the constant bullying he had been facing at school. He describes himself as not the most outgoing person before he was on social media. It would seem that he found himself via the camera lens he used.

In the same year, his single peaked at number ninety on the Hot 100 and Google declared him to be the ninth-most-searched musical artist of the year. His solo mini-tour of six cities in 2016 was followed by another tour of seven countries in 2017. By then, he had released two more singles—" Hit or Miss" and "All My Friends"—and his debut extended play record, *The Last Text* EP. The EP figured at number seventy-two in the US. In 2018, Jacob released another EP titled *Better With You*. Currently, his official TikTok profile has over 23.8 million followers.

One of the biggest pieces of advice that Jacob gives his fans and followers is to stay down-to-earth and be themselves. He says that one's aim must be to make a change in society or the area he has chosen professionally and not to get personally bigger or make money. This is also perhaps why he says he likes hanging out with friends he knew way back before he became famous. They are the ones, along with his family, who keep him grounded. When asked about why he thinks he made a splash on social media, he attributes it to his unflagging energy levels and his penchant for understanding and having fun with lyrics. In his heart, Jacob believes himself to be more of a musician than a performer, and that's what he has been focusing on over the last couple of years (Nagi, 2016).

Apart from making videos and music, Jacob has lent his support to social causes. For instance, he took part in and spoke at the March for Our Lives protest in favor of gun control legislation in Los Angeles in 2018. He has also used his social media handles in the past to speak openly about issues such as bullying, among others.

With his heart in the right place and a song on his lips, let's hope that Jacob conquers the world in all the right ways!

Jackie Evancho

Jacqueline Marie Evancho's inspiration to sing came after watching the film, *The Phantom of the Opera*. Though she sang at home, her parents did not notice anything out of the ordinary until she entered the Kean Idol talent competition at the age of eight, where she won second place. After that, she started taking voice lessons and participated in a number of events right from the local church choir to the annual school musical. She also started a YouTube channel, which garnered some attention.

2009 was the year that the world actually saw and heard Jackie. She came second in the fifteenth annual U.S.A. World Showcase Talent Competition, and once again second in Kean Idol. Around the same time, she caught the attention of record producer, David Foster. The same year saw the release of her first solo album, *Prelude to a Dream.* It consisted of fourteen song covers for classical crossover songs, a few of them in Latin and Italian as well.

In 2010, after two unsuccessful auditions, Jackie got selected for NBC's *America's Got Talent.* She eventually finished 2nd on the show. The final episode got over 16 million viewers and was one of the highest-rated finales. In fact, many viewers were convinced that Jackie should have won. Be that as it may, she was catapulted into the national limelight and went on to release several more albums in addition to her earlier debut. Her albums have crossed a record sales of over 2.2 million.

She also has a series of firsts in her name. She is the youngest solo platinum artist, which means she is the youngest artist to have over one million records sold. She is the highest-ranking debut artist of 2010, and the youngest debut artist to appear in the U.K. Top Five, and the youngest person to give a solo concert at Lincoln Center. All her albums have hit the number-one spot on the Billboard Classical chart as well. In her short career span, she has also collaborated with the greats of music like Barbara Streisand, Fernando Varela, Placido Domingo, Peter Hollens, and Joshua Bell—just to name a few. Jackie has been featured in *Billboard* magazine's 21 Under 21: Music's Hottest Minors in 2011 and 2012 and *Forbes*' 30 Under 30 list of musicians in 2018.

What stands out about Jackie is her humility and unflinching honesty. Recently, she spoke about her seven-year-old love-hate relationship with food. She has been battling anorexia for years and is currently undergoing therapy to beat it. Though she had been diagnosed with an eating disorder in the past, her greatest impetus to fight it was stirred after a car crash she survived in 2021. Her bones were so weak and brittle that she suffered major breaks at two spots in her back. That is how she realized that her poor eating had triggered osteoporosis as well.

Jackie's courage in being able to talk of her health problems in the glaring light of media attention, and her undying passion to not let the *blood, sweat, and tears* she has put into her career go to waste owing to it, is praiseworthy. We hope that Jackie can heal her scars to continue making the spell-binding music that we associate with her.

Conclusion

At the start of this book we asked the question, 'Is the secret to the success of these entrepreneurs something innate, or can it be learned?' We wondered whether those with natural talents were predestined to become entrepreneurs, and asked, If you do not have the innate qualities needed, can you ever succeed as an entrepreneur? After looking at each of the 37 stories in this book, I think it could be argued that the success that leads to the creation of a successful young entrepreneur is both an innate talent and a learned trait.

The vast majority of the kids and teenagers in this book have a personality that lends itself to being open-minded and they are all able to see the bigger picture. These young entrepreneurs understand that possibilities for business are all around us. They see gaps in markets that need to be filled, and they know that those gaps do not always need to be filled by new inventions or strategies; rather just by doing something different with what is already available. Most young entrepreneurs also have a deep sense of creativity, which can take many forms, be they practical or intellectual. These individuals see the world differently from most of us. They can imagine new realities and work and have outstanding problem-solving.

These young entrepreneurs also had to develop skills, or are still developing, they journeyed toward success. Examples include dealing with stressful situations and how best to approach those things or people who may make them feel incapable. They have also had to learn about each of their respective fields, putting in the time and research to understand their passion or field of study better.

These particular entrepreneurs also had to learn how to deal with people's unfair judgment of their abilities. Each of them started their path to success at a life-stage where most people have little to no understanding of business. Sometimes adults viewed them – or indeed still view them – as incapable of running a business or of handling large sums of money, because of their youth.

What is apparent in each of the stories we have looked at is that each young entrepreneur has not journeyed toward success alone. They have all had some form of support around them. Some of them have parents, who have walked the path closely with them, going with them to board meetings, filming them, or giving them start-up money. Others have had friends who have worked alongside them, taking on the same burdens and sharing in their successes or failures. Still others have had mentors to give them advice and guidance, and who have helped them without interfering or taking credit.

For anyone reading this book, who wants to start out on their own entrepreneurial journey, it is very important that you think about what you read in this book and take four crucial lessons away with you.

First, you need to be willing to take risks. You will never be 100% certain of the future. If you were you might not take the opportunities you have been given, and someone else may benefit from your lack of courage. Second, do your research. You need to understand the product or service you will be putting out into the world and to have in-depth knowledge about your target market. Third, you need to realize that – more often than not – success does not happen overnight. You have to be willing to wait for it and to continue working hard to achieve it, even when it feels as if the hard work is not paying off. Lastly, you must be ready to deal with failure. Many of the stories we read were about young entrepreneurs who tried various other businesses, before they found the one that brought them success and money.

If you can see the lessons in these stories, then I suspect you may be ready to start your entrepreneurial journey!

Thank You for Reading Millionaire Kids.

Hi there!

Big thanks for reading our book. We're delighted to share the magic of "Millionaire Kids" with you.

Did you like the book? If you did, can you help us out? We'd be super happy if you could leave a review. This helps more kids and families find our books and enjoy them just like you did. To leave a review, simply scan the QR code below or head over to our website at booksbycooper.com/millionairekids.

SCAN ME

Every review means a lot to us. Thank you for helping our small business grow!

Your friend,
Cooper

Made in United States
North Haven, CT
23 June 2024

53951962R00085